New Life Clarity Publishing

205 West 300 South, Brigham City, Utah 84302
https://newlifeclarity.com/

New Life Clarity Project can send authors to your live event.
For more information or to book an event contact New Life Clarity
Project at **newlifeclaritypublishing@gmail.com**
Printed in the United States of America

ISBN/SKU:9780578549620
ISBN Complete:978-0-578-54962-0
Copyright: Ulrich Floresca @2019

I dedicate this book
To YOU.

As we sip our coffee or tea, before we head off to work, or as we sip our glass of wine before bedtime, let's read together.

I dedicate this book to all individuals and their stories, whether those stories are heroic or mundane. You inspired this book. From my cup to yours, mug to mug, to the clinking of bottles or glasses, in the wee hours of the morning or the middle of a sunny day, let's toast to our own humanity. Let my story be a balm of comfort.

May we all become someone who allows transformation to take place. May we all lift those who have fallen along their journey. Cast aside the debris that drags us down and let us celebrate the power of humankind.

Zer0 Debris

A Way of Life

***

Book 1

ULRICH FLORESCA

ZER0 DEBRIS

A Way of Life

What started as a beach cleanup became so much more.

3 Countries (and Growing), 1 Mission, 0 Debris

Our mission is to clean trash and debris which are harmful to all living organisms, from the shorelines of oceans, seas, lakes, and any body of water that has life in it. We are a group of individuals who will continue this mission until we rid the beaches of all forms of contaminants. Until they are ZERO DEBRIS. To touch, move, and inspire the world as to what a clean shoreline can do and how it can benefit not only our humanity but also the marine life who co-exist with us and from whom we get our sustenance.

Wave of Contents

Foreword

There are ideas, thoughts, and desires in our heads we push aside. We say "NO" to the possibility of change before we even begin to process what it means to change. We self-sabotage ourselves, despite the fact that, as human beings, our only goal is to survive. We are the ones holding ourselves back, our own worst critics.

We tell ourselves that anything out of the ordinary is a myth, when in fact, a legend. Zero Debris is a myth, and Zero Debris is also a legend created by legendary men and women with hearts that love, who give generously to all humans.

What does it take to free ourselves from the trivial debris, waste, trash, and rubble of daily life? Well, turn this page and together, we'll find out.

"If each person cleaned the debris from within themselves; our world would be filled with people who are loving, generous and kind." ~ *Ulrich Floresca*

Start.

On November 16, 2018 my friend Abigail posted on social media: "I am wondering if I know anyone who would love to finish and publish their books in the next three months? Comment or message me!"

A few hours after it was posted, there were two likes, one wow, and thirteen comments. The first comment was bravely posted.

He said: "Make that six months."

The book was going to be titled The Mermaid Who Gave Up Her Fins. Little did the original poster know, that this guy was for real. So, he bought a laptop and type away as he is doing now, fifteen days after posting that update. He wanted to write about a mermaid. But not just any mermaid. The ONE, the mermaid for him.

His mermaid, who would trade her fins for legs so she could walk along the beach from sunset to dawn.

Why a mermaid? Well, everyone has been talking about unicorns, or the "Blonde" with three dragons, hungry for a casted metal cold throne. Winter was near, when this book was written. Then a striking realization hit him, an epiphany:

WHY?

Why would a mermaid trade her fins for him? You see, this mermaid has been swimming her whole life, and she was curious about the world. There are definitely Mermen in her world, but maybe she wanted something else; perhaps the monotony of her life underwater gave her the strength to seek someone, or something, else on the surface.

She swam to the surface, on a cold December morning, and saw two men trying to do an impossible task: pick up trash and debris along the shorelines. She watched these men, smiling, curious to discover what they were trying to accomplish.

These men were not only attempting an impossible task, but they were having fun doing it!

The mermaid looked at her fins and wished, more than anything, that she could walk with them and help them pick up the seemingly endless amounts of garbage cluttering the shore.

She waited patiently for the full moon to rise. This is the most mystical time of the night, as this is when mermaids were able to walk on land, and she walked, clothed with a garment not seen before. She looked for the men, but couldn't find them. Days passed, she continued searching, but she never found them again. She hoped to see them again, one day.

****

After searching that beach for a month, she saw a group of eleven people cleaning trash off the shore. Among that group, she finally saw the man she had been looking for. She approached him, introduced herself, and the man explained what his group was doing.

She felt happy. At that moment, their eyes glistened with delight, a tachycardic moment as they both smiled at each other.

"Do you believe in mermaids?" she asked. "Are you familiar with the nymph goddesses of the ocean?"

"Yes," he nodded. He never dreamt of meeting a red-haired woman with such deep blue eyes. Her skin radiated, her toes curled in the sand, her voice was a soft melody that captivated him.

He was an average man: spiky, salt and pepper hair. There was nothing extraordinary about him.

"I have been hearing something," she said, "and I wanted to ask if it was okay for me to place my hand on that sound."

"What sound?" he asked, frowning.

She extended her hand and placed it on his chest. "This," she explained, "is what has been making that strange sound, and it's thunderous, beating louder than the waves."

He touched her hand upon his chest and said, "This is what we call a heart."

The man stood in disbelief. On this beach was a beautiful, mystical woman who was captivated by his extraordinary glow. How could this be real?

Imagine what it would be like - inviting her clan and his clan to a wedding of the century, where a myth meets a legend. The wedding would be spectacular: A bride half-submerged in the ocean, her family and friends also submerged, dolphins holding up the seaweed veil, while he wore a scuba jumpsuit. Floating on a raft. Then his guests and family would be dining along the shore.

Definitely no fish crabs or shrimp on the menu. The merriment would be amazing, and it would be a euphoric celebration; a union of two different worlds. The ocean waves would play live music.

After the ceremony, human frailty would once again reveal itself: all the trash would be left behind, discarded irresponsibly along the sand. That would be the first major discourse between the human family and the mermaid clan. That's why mermaids became a myth for humans, the same way humanity became myth to them.

Her father, the king merman, ordered the breakup of the event, and that no mortal shall ever be able to leave that area alive. He spoke in an angry tone. "My kingdom has provided you with sustenance. We have been lenient and generous to you land-walkers, and this is how you repay us? Princess, return to our kingdom. Return to your rightful home. This man and all his clan are not to be associated with."

The groom stood, armed with love for his woman, and pleaded, "Your majesty, I request you not be hasty. I understand you're upset with how my clan irresponsibly trashed the beach. I understand you're disgusted with the disrespect we have shown. I understand your anger, you are right to be angry, but we can rectify this situation and come to an agreement."

"What agreement?" The king narrowed his eyes. "This has been going on for centuries. It is impossible to change human nature, and I am no longer interested in empty words and false promises."

"I understand your concern," the groom replied. "There has been a broken promise between our clans. My clan is responsible for breaking that promise, and I humbly stand before you with only one intention: uniting our worlds. I give you my word that I will keep my promise to clean these beaches, rain or shine, even if it means I am the only one doing it."

He watched the king, looking for a reaction, but the king responded only with silence.

"It can be done," the groom continued. "My fellow humans will do everything they can to fulfill the promise we have made."

For the first time, the king was taken aback. He had never before met a human who spoke from his heart.

****

My book in three pages.

Stop!

Alright, Okay, okay, okay... maybe not a king, because after all, that would make the mermaid royalty.

But why not make the mermaid royalty? This is my book, and I am the one telling the story.

THAT, MY DEAR READERS, is a story. The debris on the shorelines is not.

Plastic bottles float along the coasts of several seaside countries. Marine life faces extinction due to the garbage floating across the world's oceans.

And it's all thanks to us: you and me. We are indifferent to the damage we inflict upon this planet. That, my dear readers, is non-fiction.
This book is not about myths and legends, like dragons, unicorns, or even the mermaids I spoke of.

What is the reason this book was written, you ask? Am I a pretentious fraud trying to sweep a woman off her feet, or am I doing this as an act of sanctimonious self-congratulation? Am I being a rebel with a cause? Is this a fad? The answer to all those questions is a loud, resounding NO.

No, sir. No, ma'am. This is coming from a place of kindness and love.

I hope you are beginning to see who I am in relation to my word, and who you are as members of the human race. This is a call to action.
This, ladies and gentlemen, is my true self. This is who I am, and this is how Zero Debris has impacted my life.

To write this book and share with the world what a life lived with complete FREEDOM - no boundaries, no self-filtering masks, and no filth within us. How would that look?

I am living a life I love, a life filled with generosity of spirit, authenticity, and adventure.

I am writing this to inspire my readers, to push you to take action, and to touch our hearts with love. Be courageous enough to clear, clean, to toss aside, and to make sure it is disposed of properly. All the trash, impurities, filth, junk, rubbish, crap, garbage, rubble is to be eradicated. Does that sound like an impossible task? Yeah, maybe so. But we can still try. We have nothing to lose by trying.

Which brings me to ask myself: what promise did I make? I promised to clean and clear my being. I promised the possibility of a clean beach, a clean shoreline, sparkling oceans, lakes, rivers, and canals so that there is… Zero Debris.

The phrase "Zero Debris" is a term that, as I reflect on it, offers unfathomable possibilities that stretch wider than the reach of my arms.

It began as a challenge, a dare of sorts, and it showed me who I truly am. It showed me who I could become, and it taught me to hold my head up high in the face of defeat.

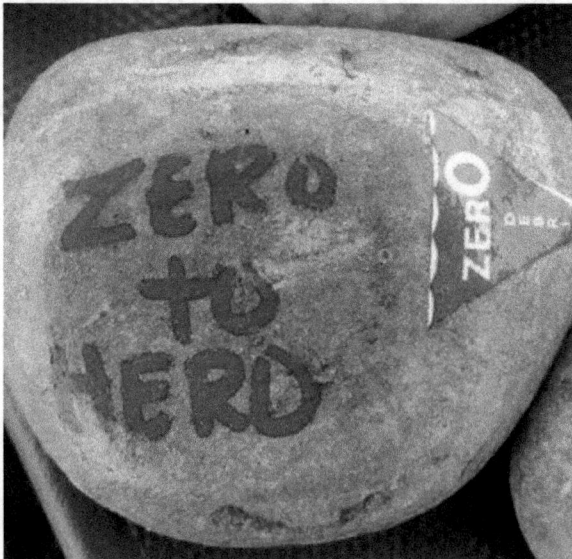

Ripple 1

There Were Two Gentlemen

2017

2019

Who Started An ACTION

Chapter 48

DEBRIS – A Life In Turmoil

December 8, 2017: I was drinking my morning coffee at my favorite local coffee shop, while trying to figure out what to do for my birthday. I would be turning forty eight years old, and the voice in my head kept whispering, "Throw out a party! Invite that woman you've got your eyes on. Introduce her to your boys. Make merry. Have fun. Drink up. And why not? You only turn forty eight once. You've earned this!"

Seven years ago, following my divorce, I didn't have a stable job. I didn't own a house. I had no money in the bank. I rattled around town in a rusted, beaten up junker of a car. I spent my time wallowing in bitterness, self-pity, and resentment.

Oh yeah, that makes sense, I scolded myself. Splurge a little, huh? Splurge on some ridiculous party when you don't even have gas money? Splurge on a date when your car can't even travel down the freeway without breaking down?

Well, that was 2012, and I thought my life was in turmoil. I spent several years living that way. Too many years.

As I continue to sip on my coffee. Still seated down, that morning of December 8th 2017, I decided to turn myself around. I posted something on social media, an announcement: "On my birthday, I am going to do 48 acts of love and kindness." I planned to visit the sick, feed the ducks at Balboa Park, give blankets to the homeless. That post on social media earned a decent amount of likes. My friends appreciated my willingness to step outside of myself and help others.

I asked a good friend, mentor, and leadership coach, a woman named Judy Lee, to define what a selfless act of love and kindness would be.

"Go to the beach," she replied, "and pick up empty bottles, cans, and every piece of garbage you see."

I thought that was a fantastic idea. I posted again on social media: "Who wants to go to the beach with me and pick up some empty bottles?"

One friend of mine replied with a very enthusiastic "I am down, bro!"

This friend was Hamid, a rugged, dashing Mediterranean man in his mid-twenties, sporting a large, healthy mane and a very fashionable beard. He has dark brown eyes. He's soft-spoken, but passionate. We met in one of the many personal and development courses I've taken.

At 7:30am, I met with Hamid at Pico and Ocean in Santa Monica. We brought with us five pairs of gloves and five trash liners. As we walked along the streets, en route to the beach, we started picking up trash. I thanked Hamid for his time and generosity. He was the only friend who had offered to join me that day.

Almost 80 paces from the beachfront, we encountered two female joggers dressed in tights and a tank top, one blonde and blue-eyed, the other brunette.

"Oh my, you guys are doing an awesome job," said the brunette.

"Yeah, keep up the good work!" the blonde encouraged.

After those lovely joggers passed, I looked at Hamid. He looked back at me. Neither of us could contain our gleeful laughter.

We high-fived. We thought we were pretty sly.

"Bro, chick magnet," Hamid said.

"Yeah, better than babies and puppies," I replied.

We fell silent for a few moments. The smiles faded. The laughter stopped. We stood in quiet contemplation.

"What if we do this once a month?" Hamid asked. "And what if we invited others to join us?"

"Yeah, that's an awesome idea, bro," I said. "Let's go for it. Let's clean this beach up until there is zero debris."

The words left my mouth before I even realized what I was saying. I realized that I possessed the power to create. I came to the sudden realization that my life was not in turmoil, as I once believed. It just needed a shift. What can I create? What could I give? How could I contribute to expansion of my being? How can I change my thinking? How can I become what I know I am capable of becoming?

Cleaning up the beach debris was only the first step; it was act one in my plan to commit 48 Acts of Kindness.

O Admin · December 11, 2017 ·

Hi COMMUNITY!!! Im turning 48this December 27th..

I have a project! For EXTRAORDINARY work- from extraordinary community

Its called (See photo)

So Please pitch in Your IDEAS!
... less $$$ .. more generous actions!!!
... (Please comment Your idea and i Will Add it on the list) Love You

48 HUMANITARIAN Acts of Love and Kindness

1. Visit the sick   2. Give socks/throw blanket to the

Chapter 47

UNFAIR: The World is Unfair

I've been divorced since November 2012. For several months after that, I took solace in a bottle of Jack and Coke. I was tipsy by 6am. I brushed my teeth, then drank a shot of whiskey before heading to work. I stopped at a fast food joint and bought a $1.00 sandwich and a $1 large iced coke. I poured more Jack into the coke. Such was my diet during the first year after my divorce.

During my lunch break, I went to a nearby supermarket and bought a rotisserie chicken. I had half for lunch and saved the second half for dinner.

I was hateful. I hated everything and everyone. I cursed all the time. I was merely surviving. The world is unfair, I told myself. It's not my fault. None of this is my fault. Why is this happening to me??? Woe is me. Come, everyone, please have pity on me. And so on and so forth.

I am a licensed dentist. I was also a college professor for three years. I had a good practice and had patients who loved my knowledge and skills.

In 2010, I was hired for my first job in the USA. I was a window washer at a large, four-story building in Pasadena. At the time, I hated it. I hated that job with a passion. I complained literally my entire shift, from the time I clocked in to the moment I finally, blessedly clocked out. It paid $50 for eight hours.

Unfair? You bet. The world is unfair. That was how I saw it.

My fault? Of course not. Absolutely not. I've done everything I can. It's not my fault. It can't be. It must be someone else's fault, everyone else's fault. It must be.

Or so I thought.

Oh, the debris of arrogance! The debris of self-righteousness! The never-ending burden of always being right!

I didn't need to complain about my lousy window-washing job. I didn't need anyone to feel sorry for me, and I definitely didn't need to shoot back Jack and Cokes during my morning commute to work. What I needed was to look inside myself, discard my own debris, and find out who I really was underneath that mess.

But I wasn't quite ready to do that work. Not yet.

I look at who I am then, and who I am now, and I tell myself, that is not who you are, anymore.

Look within you and discard that debris and see what opens up.

What is fair?

Chapter 46

BLIND: I Cannot See

*B*eauty is in the eye of the beholder. That's how the expression goes.

What beauty can we see in one another if each and every encounter is pre-judged? Evaluated? Measured?

No wonder we can't really see what is in front of us. I certainly couldn't see any beauty in anything washing windows in Pasadena for fifty dollars an hour. This is the debris of judgement. We have already decided that something (or someone) is ugly before we've given ourselves a chance to really see.

For years, I denied myself the possibility of experiencing anything beautiful. I wasn't blind. Rather, I was pretending to be blind.

It was easier to pretend to be blind, rather than taking a good, hard look at myself.

Instead of walking along my inner shoreline and picking up the junk, picking up the empty bottles, soda cans, the sandwich wrappers, and the contaminants, I looked the other way. Other people had made a mess out of me, I thought. Not me. Certainly not me. At the time, I didn't care to change myself, and I didn't care to change my world around me.

The blindness in me prevented me from seeing what I could do, who I truly was, what I was capable of doing.

Of course, I was not really blind. After all, I had (and still have) a good working pair of eyes. But at that dark time in my life, I only saw what I wanted to see. I saw things not as they were, but how I wanted them to look. I would twist the facts, I would twist logic, until it supported the reality I invented.

The eyes are the windows to a person's soul, right?
What window is there to look into if my heart is filled with nothing except hate, blame, and resentment?

Those attitudes are nothing but useless debris brought about by past experiences. Bad judgement calls. Faulty conversations. Unresolved relationships.

Cleaning up the beach on a Saturday or Sunday morning once a month allowed me to see that which is hidden. There is more to life than the self-centered coziness of one's bed.

There were months, even years, where I asked myself, "What the heck are you doing? It's Sunday, go back to bed. Rest. Sleep in."

It took me 48 years before I really looked at the man staring back at me in the mirror. It took 48 years before I really saw him for who he could be, if he tried, and not just who he thought he was.

That man wanted, just wanted to be happy. Nothing more, nothing less. It was that simple.

As bitter as I was, I was still a human being, capable of loving and being loved. I just did not want to see it that way. At least not yet. Because...

Chapter 45

EXCUSES: Because

*B*ecause. That word was powerful enough to keep me from doing anything positive. It was potent enough to prevent me from accomplishing anything even remotely positive or selfless. I was full of excuses. I had an unending supply of them.

"I don't have enough time." "I'm busy." "I cannot deal with that right now." "I have no money." "I have something important to do." "I just don't have time for you." "I am emotionally unavailable." I repeated these excuses so often, over and over again, until I eventually started believing my own lies.

It makes sense that I made those excuses. No one wants to be accountable for something, but we must be.

This debris on the beach - whose is it?

All the bottles, cans of beer, plastic utensils, plastic cups, napkins, balloons, styrofoam cups, paper plates - who did they once belong to?

Hypodermic needles and syringes. Getting high on a beach during sunset. Psychedelic colors. Whoa! Why not? Woohooo!

Used condoms. Tampons. Clothes. Shoes. Everything discarded. Irresponsibly.

I made so many excuses, in order to avoid cleaning up my own trash.

I sounded like an eight-year-old, a child throwing a little temper tantrum because he didn't want to pick up his mess. If I had listened, if I had cleaned up my own mess, I would have been able to focus myself on what really mattered. I would have been able to live a new life, become a brand-new person. I would have heard the knock of fresh opportunities on my front door.

But I didn't hear opportunity knocking. Of course I didn't. How could I, when I was too busy making excuses?

Chapter 44

BLAME: Who Is At Fault

*M*y marriage ended, but it was all her fault. Right? Of course it was. I certainly never would have accepted any blame. Not back then, at least.

I work my butt off to provide, and it seemed to me as if it was never enough for her.

I was tired of the bickering, of the nagging questions. Not my fault. I provided a decent home, a decent living, I made decent money, I took care of the kids, took jobs that were not even for my profession, just to make ends meet. We even had two housekeepers who made it easier for us to deal with home management.

We cared for our housekeepers. We never treated them as if they were servants. We were friendly, respectful. They joined us when we ate, or if we wanted to see a movie. eating. We gave them as much time off as they needed, depending on what was happening in their lives at the moment.

One of our housekeepers even told me, "Kuya, kahit walang sweldo, basta ikaw ang amo, ok ako," which translates into: "Big brother, even if I don't have salary, as long as I am with you, and you're the one in charge, I am ok."

I spent so many years denying that anything was ever my fault. I spent so much time insisting that if anything negative happened in my life, it wasn't my fault. I assumed someone else was to blame.

Then, slowly but surely, I started shifting my perspective. It wasn't easy, and it didn't happen overnight, but it gave me a way to see that often, it was in fact my own fault. If I screwed my life up somehow, if I made a mess of things, I started accepting the blame, rather than blame someone else.

I took responsibility for how my life evolved, for the good as well as the bad. I finally took responsibility for my marriage ending. My excuse for years was something like, "Well, don't look at me, it's not my fault." But that was changing.

It was much easier to blame the people around me than it was to accept responsibility, but that's what I did. I accepted full responsibility.

For so long, I was self-centered, proud, and egotistical. I didn't care who was hurt by my actions. If they had been hurt by something I did, I just assumed it was their own fault.

But that was transforming. My attitude was changing.

In November 2015, I was attending another self-improvement course, learning and understanding what agreements were.

One Saturday morning, even though we hadn't spoken for a while, I picked up the phone and called my ex-wife: "Hi, it has been a while, hasn't it? Like five years?"

"Yeah," she replied. "It has been. Do you have a girlfriend now?"

"No, I don't have any girlfriend."

She chuckled. "That's because you are still hung up on me, isn't it?"

I cursed and hung up on her.

I walked back into the classroom and took my seat. When the coach asked the class who wanted (needed) coaching, I raised my hand without hesitation.

The leader coach called on me, asked me to share. I shared the conversation I had just had with my ex-wife.

At the end of my angry rant, the coach waited for a moment. Silence. When he finally spoke, he said, "Are you ready?"

"Yes, Coach, I'm ready."

"Call your ex-wife back. Immediately. Tell her you still love her. Tell her she's right, that you're still hung up on her." His tone was smooth and gentle, but I was furious. I cursed him out too, the same way I cursed my ex-wife.

"Watch your language," he warned. Then he was silent. For several moments. It was a squirmy, uncomfortable silence.

He finally spoke: "Ulrich," he said, "what did you promise her when you were at the altar getting married?"

My jaw dropped, and of course, I didn't want to answer the question. I knew he was going to find some way to blame me. I knew he was going to try to make me accept some kind of responsibility.

Finally, I answered him. "I promised," I said, "that I would love her until death do us part." By this time, I was bawling uncontrollably. "But coach, she's married now. I don't want to tell her I love her. She'll think that I haven't moved on. She'll think I'm some loser who never got over her."

The coach smiled and looked around the class. "Does anybody from this group want to assist him when he makes the call?"

I didn't want to accept anyone's help. They had good intentions, loving intentions, but I knew this was something I had to do on my own. I called my ex-wife back.

"Hi," I said. "I'm sorry for hanging up on you a while ago. That was rude. The truth is, I broke my word."

"Huh?"

My voice shook. "I promised that I would to love you until death do us part. I broke my word. I apologize for cheating on you behind your back. For years I blamed you, but I know now that it was my fault. I do love you. That's the truth, even though I cannot love you physically, emotionally, or financially. Thank you for giving us three amazing, adorable children."

When I finished, I waited for her to answer, but the only thing I heard was her crying, followed by a soft "Thank you."

Then she hung up.

It took a lot of courage for me to do that. After the call, I felt free.

For the first time, I felt true freedom. And all I had to do was take responsibility for my own actions. I felt as if I had purged myself. I didn't need to sweep any debris under the rug. It was time to man up.

The debris of blame and blaming had been eradicated. I finally learned how to be responsible for my own choices. I knew how to take accountability. That beach had been cleaned.

Chapter 43

LIES: White Lies, A Little Hidden, Bent

*I*n the spring of 2016, I was dating someone new. She was a blonde. I've always had a soft spot for blondes. The relationship was new; we had only gone out three or so times at this point.

One day, we were getting ready to go out for dinner, and she asked me the question that every man is afraid to hear:

"Do I look pretty," she asked, "or do I look fat in this dress?"

"No, hun, of course you don't look fat," I told her. "You look..." I swung my head side to side. "...You look amazing."

"Liar! This is so shitty," she said.

I should have stopped there. I should have kept my mouth shut and taken the easy way out. But I didn't.

"Okay," I said, "since you want the truth, yes, you do look bloated, but still very pretty, hun. Do you want to change into something more comfortable?"

She changed her outfit. She changed into something much more comfortable: pajamas. Then she called off our dinner date.

I considered that a trick question. Was there any good way I could have answered? What truth did she want to hear? My truth? Her truth? I had no idea.

After that incident, I asked a female friend for her opinion. "What should I have said? Is there any good way to answer that question?"

"If a woman ever asks you that question again," she said, "try replying with 'Why, hun? Is there something else that you want to wear?'"

Well, as the old song goes: "I'd rather hurt you honestly than mislead you with a lie."

Several years ago, I sent a bouquet of flowers to a woman. When she received them, she called and thanked me. I heard the surprise and gratitude in her voice.

Then she asked: "Are you hitting on me?"

I chuckled.

She chuckled too. "Well, thank you for thinking of me. But, Ulrich, I should probably tell you that I already have a boyfriend." She paused. "I really love the flowers, though."

"You're welcome," I said. "I'm glad you love the flowers."

We were silent for a few seconds.

"I hope you're okay with me being straight-up about this," she said.

"Of course I'm okay with it," I said. But that was a lie.

After the phone call, I started beating myself up. What the fudge did you do this time? You're such a dork! You really should not have done that. I face-palmed so hard, just like the SMH emoji.

I promised myself I'd tell the truth, and the idea that transformed my entire attitude was that I was responsible for how I behave, and whether or not I'm honest with people. The woman with the flowers had been straight-up with me, but I had not been brave enough to be straight-up with her.

From that moment on, I promised myself that no matter what, I would be completely honest with everyone. I decided not to let fear prevent me from telling the truth, even if that truth was uncomfortable.

"Do you swear to tell the truth, the whole truth and nothing but the truth?"

Yup. So help me God.

Chapter 42

SHAKING MY HEAD: Disbelief

*W*hen I started my Zero Debris mission, I had no idea how it would turn out, what form it would take. I had no idea how to start my own non-profit organization.

It was May 2018. I was driving to Santa Monica Pier in a state of complete disbelief. It was the 5th month of Zeroing, cleaning the shoreline of Santa Monica Pier at Lifeguard tower 20.

I looked at the team that gathered around the tent, just a handful of amazingly generous individuals. We were spread alongside the lifeguard towers 18 and 19 on the right side, and 21 and 22 on the left side. My youngest son, Dylan, was in charge of taking videos.

An architect couple from Boston, Pam and Charles, approached Hamid. Pam heartfully thanked him, and the rest of the team, for our leadership and generosity. She asked how we started this project.

My playful response was, "It's one of the forty-eight acts of kindness for my birthday. Yeah, it's true, I recently turned forty-eight, even though I look fifty-three."

Both Pam and Charles cracked up. They asked how they could contribute. I told them the paperwork was in process. Pam then gave me her number and asked me to contact her as soon as we had our 501 C3 tax number.

After they left, I had tears in my eyes. I shook my head. Years ago, when I was drinking Jack and Coke on my morning commute, I never would have believed I would be able to inspire and motivate people in such a positive way.

Fast forward to February 13, 2019. Hector, a classmate from the Benedictine School, reached out to me via instant messenger. At this point, we hadn't spoken in fifteen years.

He was a single father of two handsome young men. He had graduated as an Agricultural Engineer from the University of the Philippines. He asked me one simple question: "Bro, I know I haven't posted any comments or liked any of your posts, but I just want to know: how can I start a movement like Zero Debris?"

He told me his ideas about protecting the environment. He wanted to clean up the oceans.

I told him: "Bro, register the name ZERO DEBRIS Philippines. Do that, and we'll talk again."

He called me the next day. "Happy Valentine's, Bro, it's already being registered."

I shook my head. Wow!! Actions speak louder than words!

Hector and I communicated daily, and before either of us knew it, The Philippines Zero Debris team was born. It was officially launched on April 14, 2019.

Fast forward again to June of 2019. Hamid brought more great news: Zero Debris will start soon in Mexico! Now we were spread across three different countries! But we all had the same mission. Zero Debris.

I shook my head, when Zero debris started, I didn't know how and what it would like, to be a leader of a non-profit organization. Although I didn't know How and What.. I definitely knew my WHY?

This is the power of belief.

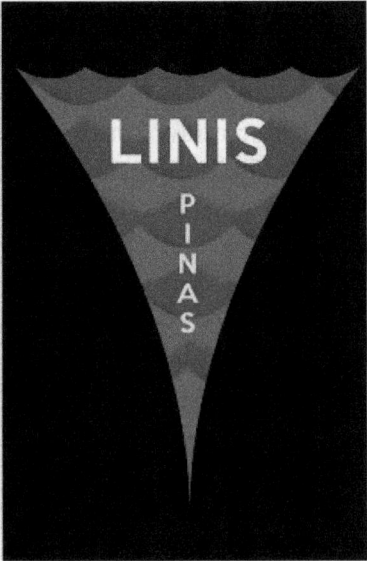

Chapter 41

LONE WOLF: It's My Way Or the Highway

Once the Zero Debris organization started picking up steam, I asked myself, Ulrich, are you up to this challenge? This is far beyond your comfort zone. What if it fails? What if it doesn't go the way you plan?

Zero Debris never had an official structure. There was never any rulebook. Like the ocean itself, Zero Debris was formless.

It was about having fun, getting people organized, and picking up trash along the tourist areas. It was about meeting the residents, the surfers, runners and joggers. It was about connecting with people who love the beach. To summarize, Zero Debris was really just about having a fun day at the beach.

I built a powerful team behind me, a loving, generous team of men and women who loved me and held me to my responsibilities as the leader of this organization.

Zero Debris allowed me to expand my thinking. It helped me realize the old saying "No man is an island" is very true. I learned that life is fun when you share your being and your passion with people who have the same passion as you do.

For a long time, my attitude towards being a leader was: "If you have an idea better than mine, keep it to yourself!" I saw myself as a lone wolf.

It took me a long time to realize that is not who I truly am, and it's not the sentiment I want to leave this earth with. That's not the attitude I wanted to pass on to my children, I wanted to show everyone my happy spirit, my crazily joyful soul.

I might have had the characteristics of a lone wolf, but it was never my true self. My Zero Debris team helped me see that I was not a lone wolf.

Instead, I was the leader of a pack.

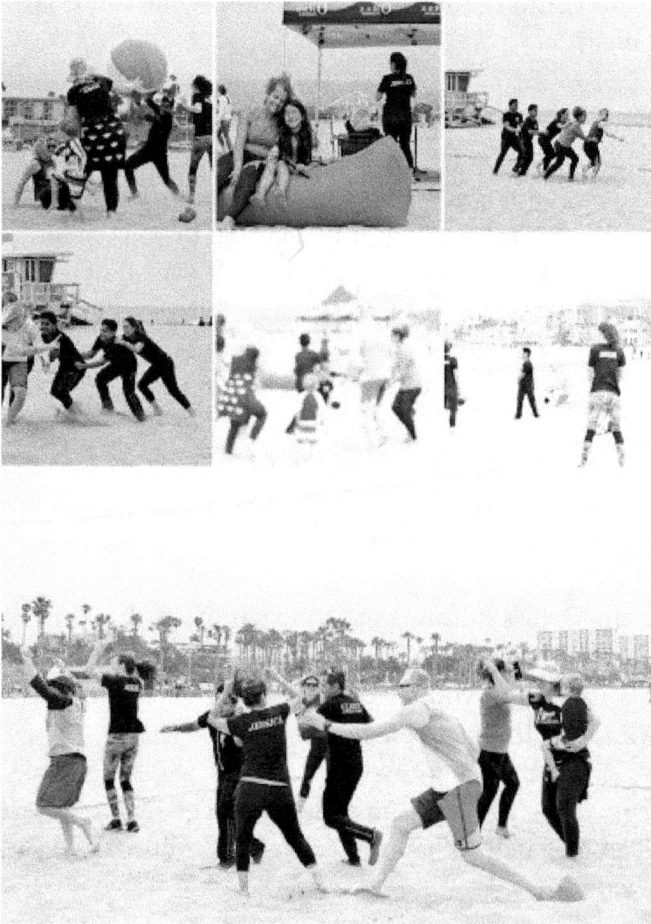

Chapter 40

BLOCKAGE: Fatty Tissue Single Use Plastic

I met a mermaid. A mermaid I affectionately named Curly Sue. She had voluptuous red curly hair, a sweet freckled face, and a warm, irresistible smile. I met her in February 2019, while standing in line to check in at the Anaheim Hilton Hotel.

"Hi," I said.

"Hi," she smiled. "Are you here for the seminar?" There was a Management and Leadership seminar happening that weekend.

"Yes," I replied. "This is my first quarter."

"Good! Welcome to the team." She asked for my name.

"Ulrich." I extended my hand.

She shook it. "Alyssa."

We sat in the hotel lobby for a while and carried on an interesting conversation, mostly about health and wellness.

She ran a project that brought awareness, support, and knowledge to stroke patients. I was mesmerized, listening intently. I was involved in the medical field and was fascinated by anything related to medicine.

What blew me away was the fact that her project translated into various languages the information about what a medical stroke is, as well as how to prevent, manage, and treat this illness. Her mission was to ensure this information was available to anyone who needed it.

The ocean needs to breathe. There are a lot of pollutants that are harmful to the marine life and the ocean water itself. There is no planet B. There is more to life than destruction. The buildup of debris in the seas and ocean needs to stop. Single-use plastic blocks the water from flowing freely. The earth will have a stroke, like fatty foods that clog human arteries.

I have a medical background. The veins, arteries, and nerves travel throughout our bodies. Imagine this gets clogged up. What happens then?

Alyssa's passion for her project, made me present in the conversation, I was focused in a way I hadn't been focused before. I gave her my complete and undivided attention. I offered to contribute to her project by helping her translate her research into into Tagalog language.

I began a new friendship that day. I stopped blocking myself off to new people, new friends or professional relationships.

I opened my heart to someone new, and it felt amazing.

Chapter 39

TRASH TALK: Sarcasm On A Sarcastic Level

I've always enjoyed a little playful sarcasm: "Which planet did you say you come from?" "Wasn't that a great meal? It cost a wing and a leg."

"Sure, it's not your trash, let's wait for the crab to pick it up and put it in the trash bin. Or maybe it's the fish, man, they had a party last night and left all this trash behind."

Human beings have a limited time on this earth, and every second counts. To participate in a trash talk is a waste of time.

It's been said that trash talk shows the wit of a man or woman, based on how quickly and smoothly a person delivers said trash talk. That idea alone is trash talk. Plastic : inauthentic, false.

The world uses several types of plastic. There are plastics that will never disintegrate. They will be here forever, even longer than humans. Our own trash will outlive us.

Take one piece of plastic and multiply it by the 7.3 billion people who use it hourly, daily, monthly, even yearly. There is an enormous garbage patch in Asia, Europe, Africa, Australia, North and South America, not to mention all the debris floating across the surface of the ocean, poisoning the water and killing the marine life.

The Zero Debris team has a saying: "It's time to stop talking trash and start picking it up."

Chapter 38

PROCRASTINATION: Lack of Action

I never would have imagined that I would write a book. I never thought it would actually happen. I was too afraid to get started. I was holding myself back from doing the work.

Procrastination might sound trivial, everyone does it, but think about this: what if my heart procrastinated in beating? What if my lungs decided to put off breathing until they "felt like it?"

The human body does not do that. The human body's primary function is to survive. It will not procrastinate. So why do we? And is procrastination synonymous with laziness? I am not lazy. I don't sit on my ass and let fate play its hand. Usually I seize the moment.

What do you think happens when you arrive late to work? The employees that were early and on time feel disrespected. Your boss will definitely feel disrespected, too.

Procrastination is the debris of being WASTEFUL.

"Huh?" you might ask. Yes. Procrastination is a debris in and of itself. Procrastination means a person is being wasteful.

No, I didn't put this off to do something else. I procrastinated because I procrastinated. Nothing wrong with that. Agreed? And that is a debris.

"What can I do," you ask, "to make sure I never procrastinate again? How can I change?" That's a great question.

I've got a great solution for you. But, I'll tell you tomorrow.

Chapter 37

HARDENED HEART: Indifferent

*T*he most basic commonality shared by every human being is that we each have a heart.

We all have hearts, but some of us choose not to use it. This is the debris of apathy, impassiveness, and indifference.

I once met a great surgeon named Dr. Bert, and we had an interesting discussion on broken-heartedness.

"Don't we love drama?" he asked. "Come with me to the operating table, and I'll open that chest of yours, just so you can show me your broken heart."

I couldn't contain my laughter. Yes, show me a broken heart, show me a scarred heart, show me a torn heart. Medically, a heart can be scarred due to muscle tear. A heart may be torn and surgically pieced together again. But broken?

In 2012, after my divorce, my male friends tried to set me up on several blind dates. They wanted me to have sex with a lot of women, hoping that it would help me get over my divorce.

Most of those dates did not turn out well, and after two grueling years of being single and intoxicated, I looked at my life and where it was headed.

It was spiraling downwards. I would talk to myself, trying to shut off the chattering in my head that never seemed to stop.

Ariadne, my daughter, once told me to "stop thinking about mom, please. Think about yourself and think about us." She told me to stop drinking because when I was drunk, I was not my true self. I was not the father she loved.

But I wouldn't listen to her. I had a hardened heart.

In Charles Dickens' A Christmas Carol, the Ghost Of Christmas Future shows Ebenezer Scrooge that when Scrooge dies, there will be no friends attending his funeral. There will be no one to mourn his death. Scrooge had a hardened heart. He didn't care about anyone else but himself.

I never wanted to be like Scrooge. I never wanted to close myself off to other people.

Things are different now.

On my daily commute from the freeway, there is a certain old man I usually see at my exit. He's holding a sign that reads: "No job, homeless, need $ to eat."

Whenever I see him, I give him all the money I can spare. I used to ask myself if I was helping him, or just enabling him? I prefer to think I was helping him.

Being generous is natural. It's in all of us. It's who we all are. No matter how hard we try to fight it, there is true joy in giving yourself to other people.

Just ask Scrooge.

Chapter 36

RULES: Breaking The Rules

I live my life by three simple rules.

Rule #1:
Do what makes you happy.

Rule #2:
Read Rule #1 and keep your word.

Rule #3:
Stop making rules.

I think three rules are enough.

The only thing about having three simple rules, is that sometimes I will come across something so important that it will cause me to be motivated enough to break my own rules.

Here's an example:

There are rules against littering. There are rules about recycling. There are rules about plastic usage. There are rules about this and that.

All of these rules are important. They need ACTION AND IMPLEMENTATION. Therefore, I have a new rule. It is to implement these rules and break my original rules.

In March 2018, I attended the third event of the beach cleanup. I was at the tent with the CFO of Zero Debris, Darren, when he asked me a question I hadn't considered before.

"Ulrich, do you know what you've created? I mean, do you know what Zero Debris means?"

"Yeah, Darren, I know," I replied.

"That space where you're standing," he said, "that sand beneath your feet - do you realize it would take a lifetime before you can totally say it has zero debris? It would take a million people to gather comb this beach until it was completely free from debris."

"I understand, Darren," I said. "I really do. We need more people to join us."

Darren wanted me to be responsible for what I was speaking and to live up to my word. He insisted that I follow through with my promises, that I follow the rules that I have invented for myself, and for my Zero Debris organization.

What Darren didn't realize was that I have almost always followed my rules to the letter. I broke my word from time to time, I'm human, I'm imperfect, but those instances were exceptions. They were not the norm.

After realizing broken a promise, I muster the guts to approach the ones I've disappointed and apologize to them. The first thing I say is, "I broke my promise." That is my responsibility. And that's how I try to approach my relationships with people.

It will take a lifetime to cause a massive transformation of the planet. The next generation of humans. So, how will WE hand over this earth to those next in line?

Zero debris: my life, your life.

Chapter 35

POWER: Manipulation, Helplessness

*W*hat comes to mind when you call someone an alpha? If a man is called an alpha, it might mean he is a leader. But if a woman is called an alpha, it might mean she is bossy and domineering. Men who are threatened by assertive women might find "alpha" to be a negative trait in a woman.

The truth is, we are all our own alphas. We are the only ones who hold power over ourselves. We are the ones who control our own thoughts and emotions. We've been given the power over ourselves.

That is why we are intimidated by ourselves. We are powerful, and that frightens us.

Puppet Master. That's a term that you might have heard before. There are a few powerful men and women who, like it or not, are puppet masters. For them, power comes from manipulation and control.

The power of control is a debris, whether you agree with me or not.

For me, an alpha male or alpha female are those who hold themselves accountable for their words and actions. A puppet master is someone who will never take responsibility for the things they say and do. The person with integrity is powerful. A person who fulfills his/her word is a powerful person.

My papa has always told me, "Son, I don't have a million tons of money. What you can rely on is my promise to you and to our family. I live on my word, and what I say is what I will do." That is his word of honor, and that word is more valuable than gold.

We all have the power to create. I have the power to create what I want my life to be. With one small act of kindness towards myself or towards the community, I can change and influence the destinies of all the people around me.

There is a story I heard several years ago. Maybe you've also heard it. It is about a boy testing an old sage's wisdom. It goes like this:

A boy quickly caught a bird and, cupping it in his hands, walked up to the wise old man and asked, "Old man, what is it that I have in my hands?"

The wise old man said, "You have a bird, my son."

The boy then asked, "Old man, tell me: Is the bird alive or is it dead?"

The wise man looked at the boy, thought for a moment and said, "Son, the answer lies in your hands."

If the old man said it was alive, the boy will squeeze the life out of the bird. If the old man said it was dead, the boy will let loose and the bird will fly away.

A powerful leader has wisdom, not answers.

POWER. It is all in YOUR hands.

Chapter 34

MONEY: Here's My Two Cents

I am fortunate to have ridden in a 1967 Ford Mustang with a vinyl top. Yes, that was the first car my family had when I was a child. It was amazing. A classic. I have four other siblings who, Thank God, are all medical doctors. I am the only dentist. My father is an attorney. My mom is an accountant.

When I was about 10 or 11 years, just a kid, my mother prepared dinner, and the family sat at the kitchen table, waiting for my father to return.

It took him a long time to come home, but when he did, he looked distraught. Unhappy. He was carrying two briefcases.

"What's the matter?" my mom asked. "You seem upset."

"I have these," my father replied, and he opened the smaller suitcases. Both cases were filled with money. He said the briefcases combined held a total of one million two hundred and fifty thousand pesos, which would have transferred over to $250,000. It was blood money, as the mafia would say.

My mom teared up right away, knowing my father was having a moral dilemma. There was a long silence.

But I, being a typical child, was only thinking about what we could do with all that money: Wow, I can ask Papa to buy the toy ROBOTS, Voltes V, Mazinger Z and Atari. We can buy a Betamax and upgrade our television!

I figured my sister probably could have her own grand piano now, rather than play the dusty old piano we had.

My parents had a serious conversation; all I could hear my mom say was "Isuli mo," which in English, translates to "Return it."

We had everything we needed. We had the essentials. We had food. We weren't starving. We weren't wealthy Filipinos, but we were doing alright. We had a Mustang. My sister and I attended private schools.

The following day, my father went back to his office and returned the money. He regretted that decision. When our financial situation became a little more strained, he was furious with himself for returning it, always saying, "I should have taken that money. We wouldn't be so hard-up!"

My mom didn't talk very much. She didn't speak up often. doesn't talk much, or argue much. When she would have serious discussions with my father about the family and about their relationship, she never said a lot. She was usually sobbing.

When I saw her sobbing, I usually came up to her and joked around with her, making funny faces or jokes until she eventually started laughing.
I did my best to cheer her up when she was sad, and I didn't need a dime to do it. I just needed my own playful personality. I just needed to be who I was. I needed to be myself, her son, and that was enough.

So, here is my two cents: Zero Debris started out as an act of kindness for Mother Earth. My team and I never asked how we would make money or turn a profit. Our mission was larger than money. Money will come and go. It's only material, made of metal and paper. The debris on the beaches, however, will always be there, unless an unstoppable team of humans stands up and makes a change.

Do you have what it takes? Come join the team.

Chapter 33

WALLS: Impenetrable

Rome was not built in a day. We've all heard this expression time and time again, haven't we?

In the fast-paced twenty-first century, a time when we are obsessed with the quick fix, the environment suffers. It takes 45 days to raise chickens. It takes nine months for a baby to develop inside a mother's womb. It takes the Earth 365 days to make a full rotation around the sun.

It takes years for someone to build a wall around themselves.

The idea in this chapter is for me to break down the walls I have built for myself to isolate myself from the rest of humanity, in defense for me to survive.

Isolation. Is that really the path I have chosen to dedicate my life to? No. I love people, and I am happy to talk with them.

So, I took the sledgehammer of love and started to smash the "impenetrable" wall I built.

Over the past four years, I have been retraining myself to see what is possible, to listen and act accordingly.

Every morning, after my shower, I look at myself in the mirror and repeat my own personal mantra: "I am a space of fun, love and excitement."

Breathe in life. Breathe out love. It's that simple.

Chapter 32

The CLOSET: What Hangs In It

*H*ave you ever heard the expression, "skeletons in your closet"?

Over my lifetime, I have accumulated more than enough clothes, shirts, jeans, dress shirts, pants, pajamas, unpaired socks, boxers and underwear that I don't wear anymore. And how about pillow cases, towels, and bedding? I have an excessive amount of clothes and fabrics in my closet.

Eventually, I finally started sorting through all the clutter in my closet. My debris, if you will.

I took everything out, one article of clothing at a time. I separated it into different categories: clothes I wear frequently, clothes I wear occasionally, and clothes that I can donate.

As I organized my closet and started giving away the clothes I no longer wear, I noticed a lot more empty space in there. My closet could breathe. The clothes in my closet could breathe as well.

I don't need a lot of clothes, I realized. Why should I have so many? There are people out there who don't even have one shirt to wear. Why should I have a closet full of clothes I never wear?

I started opening my drawers and I dumped the shelves onto my bed. Did you know I owned more than 36 pairs of socks? Trust me, I counted. I separated them into different piles, the same way I did with the clothes hanging in my closet.

I went through the same process with my underwear drawer. As I went through my clothes, my sentimental nature started to kick in. I felt the urge to stop giving so much away. I wanted to hold on to what I had.

But then I shook my head and said, "No. It's time to let go."

So that's what I did.

I didn't need any of that clutter. I didn't need all those extra clothes. They're a distraction. It made me realize what the idea of minimalism is all about: zero debris.

My closet now has a space for any woman partner who wants to join me in the future. She now has a space in my closet to call her own, if she wants.

These extra clothes, that clutter, the debris I was holding onto, were the skeletons in my closet.

Now they have been set free. Now I have let them go, and never again will they haunt me.

Chapter 31

NOT GOOD ENOUGH: I Can't

If I were to say that we are all salesmen and saleswomen, would you believe me?

The truth is, yes, we are. Every day, we are selling something.

At the office, we sell an idea. Anyone who agrees to the idea has been sold to it.

At a party or gathering, we sell jokes. We sell our very own personalities. I know I do. Anyone who laughs at the joke, sold even to the lowest bidder. The ones who chuckle silently.

We sell ourselves. For a price. The price of acceptance, contentment, comfortability, partnership.

The problem is that we, and I am including myself in this too, all secretly believe that we are not good enough. I still have days where I worry that I am not good enough to sell, not even in the bargain bin.

It took a patient of mine to prove me wrong. Her name was Michelle. She was tall, slim, deep green eyes, a Russian/Jewish woman with long hair.

For the last five years I made house calls to give her, her treatment. And while I was there, we would talk. She shared her own wisdom and ideas with me. She shared with me what is possible for me and my life, who I am, what I could become, etc.

"Rick," she said, "you should check out this weekend seminar. See what's possible. I think you'd really enjoy it."

"Oh, no, thank you," I said. "I appreciate the offer, but I don't have time and I don't have the money." Excuses, excuses.
We talked about everything. We didn't have filters when we talked. Yes, we had mouths like sailors, and we had such fun hour-long appointments, which bloomed into an amazing friendship.

Whatever the conversations were, she listened, and our conversations always ended on the subject of my love life. She introduced me to the idea of swiping left and swiping right. Hilarious.

"Rick, what are you looking for in a woman?" she asked.

"A blonde with blue eyes," I replied automatically.

"No, I mean what are you looking for in a woman?" She looked me straight through my eyes and waited for an answer.

"I dunno, Michelle, I dunno." I shook my head.

"Oh my god, Rick. You just want to get laid!"

"Well," I laughed, "isn't that what this dating app is for?"

"Yeah, but that's not all that matters. What are you committed to?"

Now that was a real talk. What are you committed to, buddy boy? Good question.

"Well," I said, "I'm looking for a relationship that is calm, drama-free, and committed to empowering ourselves as a couple. Open communication with family members, graceful conversations. Giving respect and gratitude to a higher power of being, regardless of what religion."

She finally smiled.

"This one, Rick." She pointed at a woman's profile. "Look at her. She's got nice blue eyes, brunette hair, and she's a schoolteacher. She loves hiking, rock climbing, and the outdoors. She really looks amazing and she is only 5'4" perfect for your height."

Then, I sabotaged myself.

"Nah." I shook my head. "Come on. She would not like an Asian. I'm not good enough for her. Look at her, she is gorgeous! And I'm just me."

"WTF, Rick? You really need to shift your thinking. You really need to listen to who you are. Go and check out this program in Culver City. It will help motivate you. It will give you confidence in yourself."

"Michelle, I'm okay. I have a good job, and I have my boys. I am fine, trust me."

I didn't realize it at the time, but she was selling something to me. She was selling me an opportunity to get my life and my mind back on track.

It took eight months before I finally registered to take the transformational learning course. Michelle never let up. I procrastinated to make that choice of participating in the program because of my own bullshit excuses. And once I signed up, I never looked back.

Who wouldn't want a happy life? Who wouldn't want to live with power, freedom, and ease? Who wouldn't want to live a life that they love? I know I want a life. I want a life that I love.

Because I said yes, and finally opened myself up to what Michelle was showing me, I started this Zero Debris organization.

These days, when I see my reflection in the mirror, I proudly say to him, "You are a gift to the world. You're a present with a golden ribbon bowed to your soul and this gift is offered to you whole-heartedly without inhibitions, by the Universe."

I am happy, I am worth it, and I am grateful.

 Zero Debris
@ZeroDebris

Chapter 30

TURN the PAGE: Write, Move

*T*his world is full of great storytellers. Storytellers who can make you laugh and smile. They can bring you to tears. They can make you feel excitement. They can make you ponder, reflect, and consider your own emotions.

I am a writer, just like you.

We write our stories. We read our own chapters. We share page after page after page with the world.

No matter how the world interprets the book of your life, it falls on you, the writer, to shape that story.

The readers who read my book, however, are onlookers. They bookmark pages. They write notes in the margins. They underline and highlight certain words. The other kinds of readers, the ones who don't want to hear this story, tear out the pages, fold them, burn them. Let's call them the writer's scars. They are my scars.

I have 49 chapters of my book so far. Each chapter has 365 pages. (366 pages during a leap year)

When I was fifteen years old, I walked up to my mom one time and spoke to her with conviction: "Mom, when I grow up, I will be a lawyer and run for office as a Senator."

My mom sweetly replied, "Hijo, Balong, bago ka mag senador, at maging politiko. Tumulong ka sa tao, Pag payamanin mo ang bansa. At siguruhin mo na may sarili kang pera. Para hindi sasabihin ng mga tao, kinuha mo ang pera ng bansa."

TRANSLATED: "My son, my dear son, before you run for office as a senator, make sure you help the citizens, and common men. Be patriotic and make sure your life is great, wealthy, rich, so your constituents and the mass of the people will not say you took the taxpayers money." Some true wisdom delivered to me by my mother.

I am not a lawyer. I am not a senator. I am a safe space of FUN, excitement, and love. I am Ulrich.

I am turning a new page.

Every day is a new beginning.

Chapter 29

HEAR AND LISTEN: Say That Again?

*H*USH! Listen! The smallest bone in the body is found inside the ear. The stapes. It is the stirrup bone found inside the ear that is responsible for the vibration motion.

Growing up as a boy in a Filipino family, I can still hear my mama or papa calling me, "Oist!" No matter what kind of game I was playing, I would run to heed their call because if not, they would sternly say, "Didn't you HEAR me calling you?"

I heard. Of course I heard, but because I was a kid, I didn't listen. Most kids don't listen. Most kids don't want to listen. A lot of adults don't want to listen too.

The debris of hearing, and not listening.

Listening is a tool for each one of us, to hear what is being said, and to notice what is not being said.

Look at the person you're having a conversation with, you get to hear and listen to them. Hear them talk about what they are committed to, notice the emotions hiding behind their words.

Listen to them. Listen to everything they have to offer. Everyone has their own story to share.

Listen to them and hear their greatness.

Chapter 28

TEARS: Emotional Water

The human body, as complex as it is, has a way of cleaning out pollutants.

Have you ever gotten dust in your eye? As soon as you rub your eyelids, water comes rushing out. When you have not slept properly, your eyes turn red and water droplets gush out. During moments of extreme pain, your eyes leak teardrops.

There is also emotional water that falls once you find yourself triggered by a painful memory from the past.

In November 2012, I lived in Pleasanton, a small town in Northern California. This was a period in my life when I really, really loved drama.

I was still a practicing Catholic, and every day, I went to the town church as early as 8AM. Remember, this was also the same period when I started each day with a Jack and Coke.

Every morning, I sat in the back pew, tipsy and sobbing. One morning, one of the priests noticed me, crying softly in the back row.

He approached me, a warm smile on his face. "Good morning. How are you? Is there anything that the Church can offer you?"

I pulled myself together enough to try to answer his question. "I recently had a divor..." I couldn't even finish saying the word divorce before I started weeping again.

"My son," he said, "you must allow yourself to go through the five stages of grief."

"She didn't die, Father," I replied. "She just left me. I am suffering from a divorce, not a death."

I'm sure the priest probably didn't know whether he wanted to smack me on the head or lovingly forgive me.

The priest continued. "Divorce is like death, my son. Your marriage died. You have to bury the dead and go through the five stages of grief. That is the only way you can heal."

He continued. "My son, are you crying because you had a divorce or you are crying because your ego has been hurt?"

Truer words have never been spoken.

This is the debris of pretension. Of egotism. Self-absorption. This was the real reason I was upset. My precious ego had been shattered. And this priest recognized it immediately. It was like a revelation.

After that, I finally stopped crying.

Chapter 27

TASTE: Sweet As Sugar

The taste buds at the tip of the tongue are the sweet buds. Right next to those are the salty taste buds. The sides of the tongue are the sour taste buds, and at the back of the tongue are the bitter buds. (For the record, I am a licensed dentist, okay?)

That's the reason why, when we kiss, our hearts skip a beat. It's because we're tasting the sweetness of our lover's kiss.

This is what is important in taste. What I would like to share with you is the entirety of taste. It's not just about food, it is also about life. The sweetness, saltiness, sourness, and bitterness of life.

It is just a taste. It is not the totality of our existence. In this chapter, I will be sharing my poetic side.

The next page has some of my own original poetry.

Choices

*Choose wisely
As life comes at you
Left or Right
And keep moving ahead
*Choose without reason
Never say- just so it's done
Snap out of it
Muster the guts, conquer
*Choose happily
Disregard the frown
Uncertain as is it
Anything to expand your thinking
Straddle on and get going
Set backs are nothing
It wouldn't even define you
*Choose powerfully
It's a process
Shift to a new paradigm
Needed daily
*Choose and be with it

by Ulrich Floresca * 12-18-18 * 3:03 pm

Victorious Bliss

Victorious in all life's account
No matter the odds, surmount
Happy with all smiles
Though railed with uncertainty along the aisles

Bliss amidst all stride, of noise and chaos
Ready to stand give and of pathos
Arouse the inner strength with serenity
Approach the moment with tranquility

Victorious bliss such a combination
Empower, surround, move the nation
Fully breathe in life, exhale love
Thanking the almighty above

by Ulrich Floresca * 7-29-18 * 10:10 am

I am a very intense person, to a degree not everyone understands or is comfortable with, unless the person reading these poems happens to be poetically eloquent.

"You seize the day, but never choke on the marrow of life." (John Keating, Dead Poet's Society).

The bitterness of life, most of the time we dump it. We vomit to a friend who is at first ready to listen. Then we become a broken record. The conversation loses it's flavor. Why? Because we don't want to rid the debris that we are holding onto.

The intensity of that is like eating a hot bowl of ramen. It will scald you, but the palatability and aroma is such that you would want to taste it again and again.

To enhance the flavor of food and life, the food and conversation must be savored. All of life's little flavors must be enjoyed. Slowly. Intentionally.

However, the marine life can not talk and express their sentiment.

Out of all the creatures in this world, we are the only ones who have the ability to speak.

This is real talk. I am gifted with words, and so are you, even if you don't realize it.

When we use words that are tactless, thoughtless and cause hurt for ourselves or others, it is noise pollution. And that is also a debris.

Watch your words. Live by them. Honor them. Create with them. Rejoice with them. Use them wisely.

Your words mean everything.

Chapter 26

DIVE in the DEEP: Testing the Waters

*O*n December 8, 2018, Zero Debris celebrated its one-year anniversary.

The event was called A Fun Day At The Beach with Jen H. Our organization decided to honor a woman who stands for the beauty and power of communication.

We assembled, picked up debris, gave Jen H her recognition, and offered her our gratitude. We even sang songs to her. The merrymaking was amazing.

That same day, I met another Jen. I'll call her Jen B (who agreed to be featured in this book).

There is something special about the Zero Debris event. Unless you participate and are present at the event yourself, you would think it's just a beach clean up. Well, it's not. It's so much more.

That day, Jen B attended with the love of her life, Jeff. At that event, she told me, "Ulrich, you're fun. Everyone is enjoying themselves. This is such a great project. I would like to introduce you to a friend of mine. You guys will click. Her name is Natalia."

I agreed to meet Natalia.

The New Year came and went. I was so inspired because this I had been told this woman Natalia is an outdoorswoman. A perfect fit for me.

On January 24, 2019, I drove to her home back in Lawndale. She was such a bubbly soul. There are only a few women I know who look lovely with short, neck-length hair, and with her light blue-grey eyes, Natalia rocked her look gorgeously.

She had her own way of helping Mother Earth. She had her own nonprofit organization, and her team kayaked along the harbor, picking up trash. She called her organization "Paddle4plastic."

I thought I was an outdoorsman. Nope. That day was my first time kayaking. There was somewhat of a kindred spirit connection between us. We blended nicely, like a smoothie. It was a match made in Heaven, as the old saying goes.

We paddled in our kayaks until we reached the outer rim of the Redondo Harbor. We smiled, watching happy sea lions barking and calling out to one another.

While we kayaked, Natalia told me all about how Paddle4plastic began. It started when she decided to buy a kayak of her own.

Once she bought the kayak, she took solo trips around the harbor, and she started noticing plastic floating across the water. She began picking them up. Every time she went kayaking, she picked up all the discarded trash she found out there.

This woman was pure fun. We had a great time paddling, bonding, and collecting trash.

We were up on the rocks, and I was so wet, water dripping all over from when I plunged in to get a plastic cup on the ocean floor.

We stood atop a boulder, gazing at the harbor, sharing ideas on how we can combine our projects together.

I could not resist any longer. She was too perfect, and I slowly walked up to her, my arms open to hug. She said, "Awww, that's so sweet," and she hugged me back.

By going in for that hug, I stepped out of my comfort zone. I didn't waste any time testing the waters, I just dove in headfirst without second-guessing myself. And now we go kayaking every month, cleaning up the beach, cleaning up the harbor. What began as a once-a-month-tradition now happens twice a month.

Looking back, I'm so glad I listened to Jen B. I'm so glad I agreed to meet Natalia. I'm so glad I took that dive without nervously testing the waters.

After all, LIFE is meant to be lived, not tested.

Chapter 25

EXONERATE: Acts of Kindness

*A*fter my divorce, I didn't communicate with my parents for almost four years. I finally spoke to them again, in late September 2015, the night before I was supposed to attend my first weekend seminar. I called them up on the phone.

My father answered. "Hello?, Sinu ito?" ("Who is this?") I could hear the smile in his voice.

"Pa, si Ulrich po," I replied.

"Sinu? si Ulrich?" His tone shifted and I heard him tell my mom, "O, yung anak mong divorced." Translation: "Here, your divorced son."

It had been almost four years since I last communicated with them, and a lot had happened during that time. My parents grew old and I didn't care because I'd gotten divorced. I knew my father would hate my guts.

My father handed the phone to my mom. She spoke: "Hello, olritz."

My mom was already crying as she said her hello. "Kamusta ka na, anak?" ("How are you, son?")

Upon hearing my mom cry, I started crying too. In the background I heard my father say, "Ask him what he wants. He only calls when he wants something."

Isn't that the truth? I only called my parents when I needed something.

"Anak, ok ka lang ba, may kelangan ka ba?" my mom asked. Translation: "Son, are you okay? Do you need something?"

"Yeah, mama, Ok po ako, wala po akong kelangan. Tumawag po ako dahil nasa seminar po ako, at gusto kong sabihin na, pinatatawad ko na po kayo, dahil pinatawad ko na po ang sarili ko. Salamat po sa pagmamahal"

"Yeah, Mama, I'm okay. I am attending a seminar in the morning. I don't need anything. I just called because I wanted to say I forgive you because I have forgiven myself. Thank you for your love."

My father's initial reaction was to grab the phone and ask, " Are you on drugs? Are you okay?

Despite my father's panic, I was cool, calm, and collected. I was smiling and addressed his concern, but his love was expressed differently.

"Papa, I am not on drugs. I am doing fantastic, and I wanted to ask for forgiveness, but I am also forgiving you."

He was silent, so I kept explaining: "When I got divorced, I knew you would get angry when you heard about it. And you did. I thought you hated me. I thought I was unworthy, Papa. So I didn't call you, and for that, I am sorry."

So much for cool, calm, and collected.

By the time I finished explaining myself, I was bawling. So much for cool, calm, and collected.

For the first time, I heard him say, "I love you, son." That was a big deal. He didn't actually said it, it was implied. We are Filipinos. It is in our culture not to be vocal in expressing our emotions.

"Do you need anything?" my father asked. An expression of concern.

"How are my grandkids?' He wanted news.

"Papa, mahal ko po kayo ni mama, pasensya na po kung hindi po ako tumawag at.." ("Papa, I love you and Mama. I am sorry I haven't called you"). I was in the middle of my dramatic spiel when he said:

"Anak, Pasensya na rin dahil na divorce ka, iniisp kita nun nag aalala ako sa iyo at wag kang makalimot magdasal at magpasalamat sa diyos."

Translation: "I am sorry, son, that you got divorced. I was thinking about you then and I was worried. How you were doing? Please don't ever forget to pray and give thanks to God."

He said "I love you," right? It's implied.

He expressed himself as best as he could. That is his love language.

In the legal parlance, I have been exonerated, and so has he. Forgiveness. FREEDOM.

I do not want to hold onto resentment anymore. I don't want to hold back my love for the people in my life. I want to express my love to the people that matter. I love you. I do.

Ripple 2

...And There Are Groups Of

Extraordinary Humans...

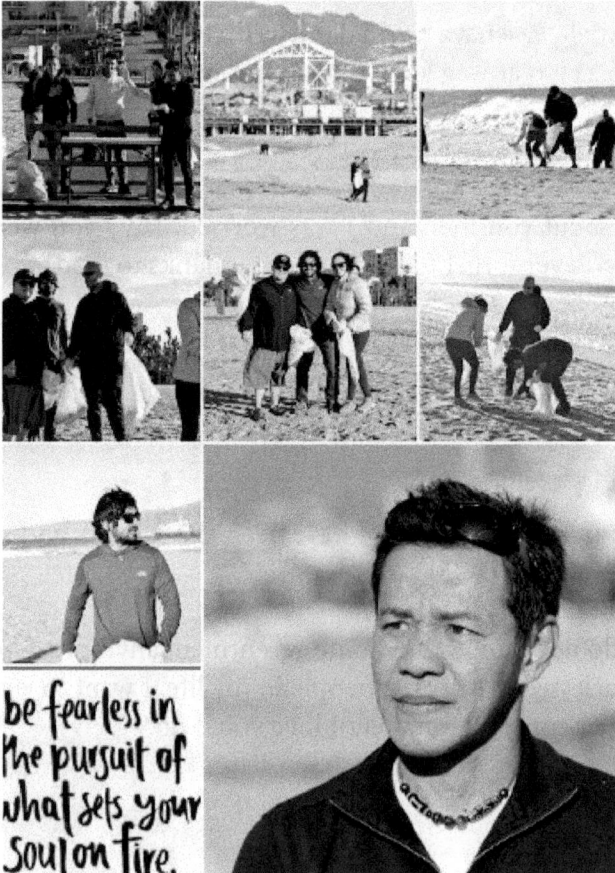

be fearless in the pursuit of what sets your soul on fire.

Chapter 24

INTENTION: Purpose

I started an act of kindness by picking up debris along the shoreline. Am I the only one who does this? Am I too proud to climb up to the top of a mountain and shout, "I am cleaning the beach?"

My intention is to pick up rubbish, and if I'm doing this to become famous or to receive attention, the act itself is rubbish.

One of the biggest flaws of humanity is selfishness, when a person does something only because they might get something out of it.

The purpose of purifying the beach, of cleaning the debris from the shoreline benefits everyone. It benefits the ocean, it benefits humanity, it benefits Mother Earth, and it benefits the creatures that live in the ocean.

There is life beneath the waves. It is a world that is serene and beautiful.

My intention is to bring awareness to what is happening to the world around us. We have a higher purpose, a higher calling, than anything we can imagine.

My purpose is to live a life with zero debris, internally and externally, and that includes having zero debris in the environment we live in.

Chapter 23

MERMAIDS: Fair Ladies

*W*hat comes to your mind when I say the word "mermaid?"

I think of a blonde, blue eyed damsel who loves the ocean. That's a stereotype, but for so many years, that's what I believed mermaids were. My belief was transformed after seeing these goddesses lovingly walk alongside me on the beach as we cleaned the garbage from the shoreline.

Mermaids are myths. The ever first mermaid in my life, however, was my mom. My mother dearest. Hailing from a northern province of the Philippines, when she was eighteen years old, she won Miss Town, standing five-foot- four inches with fair skin and long black hair that reached her ankles. She had a triangular face with prominent zygomatic cheek bones.

She was a certified public accountant, is good with numbers, and is especially good at summing, dividing, multiplying, and subtracting.

The reason I say this is that she would sum up the good I did, and subtract the bad I did, multiply my number of times getting spanked, and dividing how many days would I be whooped just for a petty childish tantrum.

She is a mermaid with a soft angelic voice. She taught me and my siblings house chores, which included going to the market, slaughtering chickens, and cutting beef in a precise way. She never had a cookbook. It was all done with love, a sprinkle of pepper and salt, a dash of cumin, paprika, and whatnot, depending on what food she was cooking.

I asked her one day, "Mama, why don't you measure the ingredients?"

She replied serenely, "You don't measure LOVE."

Today, in my Zero Debris organization, I am surrounded by mermaids.

There is Mikel, the secretary who is committed to providing proper communication, as well as a meeting recap. She towers up with her brown light reddish hair. She has a sweet smile that creates a space for you to just open up and have a conversation. A mighty wing woman, for the fact that her keen sense of intentional listening holds dearly during our meetings with supporters and viable volunteers. She is a woman who is a leader in the health department sector. She has a sweet smile that invites you to open yourself up and have a conversation.

Then there's the radiant Jessica, Vice President of the organization, hailing from south of the border. She's interested in arts and crafts. She also happens to be my dating coach. Dark sparkling eyes, long wavy hair - she has a way of lifting me out of my doldrums when I'm about to give up on everything. She is an amazing, loving, and powerful leader. Dark sparkling eyes, long nice wavy hair, salsa dancing with finesse. She has this artistic nature, with a heart to be a contribution to her local kinsmen. Her project, RADIANT, creates art. It has spread in Nepal, Peru, India.

I love Mikel and Jessica like family, but this chapter would not be complete without the mermaids I have fallen in, romantic love with.

A young mermaid, Clare, she and I had an amazing connection, yet we are on the complete opposite ends of the spectrum. She is lovely, cerebral, and seriously funny.

She is very playful, which immediately attracted me. On one of the beach clean ups, she told me what she wants to accomplish for the elderly. Well, for geriatric patients, to be medically correct.

And then there was a mermaid who didn't know I was romantically interested in her. I gave her a gift for her birthday. It was a lovely gift, very thoughtful. She appreciated it, but she told me she was already dating a guy she felt was the one. "I'm grateful for your kindness, Ulrich, but I'm sorry. I can't go out with you."

There were a few redheads. One was all over the place and didn't know what she wanted from life, even though she said she knew. Maybe she was just trying to be diplomatic and let me down easy. Who knows?

I was in Austin when I met with one of the "giants." I approached her with a smile and we exchanged pleasantries and shared tons of things. This auburn Canadian, a chocolate bar of sweetness, is authentic and real.

We spent an entire evening just creating ideas and brainstorming. She practically made me present to what I want in a woman. What's sexy to me is, a woman I can have gracious conversations with. Tickle me intellectually.

We talked about many things, including relationships. In our conversation, she said she was happy and content with who she was with. She talked about him, with eyes sparkling and a smile that couldn't be held back. I was amazed to see a woman happy and relaxed.

I want what she has. I want that kind of relationship. Freed up, eased, just in love. And I want what my father and mother have.

I thought about this and my mind said, "Clean yourself up. Keep doing what you're doing. It will all fall into place like a jigsaw puzzle."

When we were done talking, I excused myself and requested permission to put her in this book. She told me, "Yes, but make sure you don't word things in any way that would cause any issues in my relationship. I like what I have and want to keep it."

When something is brewing, don't stir it up with another ladle. Who wants to be the extra ladle, spoon, or fork in a pot or plate already being shared?

I know, for me, I do not. Been there, and the soup didn't taste palatable. And what I am committed to is to be someone's THE ONE, and be The One for someone.

Zero Debris, my debris in this aspect of life is the insatiability of what and who I want to be with.

I want more than just an animalistic, instinctual frolic with a woman. This is not the type of intimacy I want to settle for. That would be just a sex pill below the hierarchy of Maslowe's pyramid of existence.

No, intimacy comes at a proper time.

Am I filling up a void? I want to be in love with the feeling of being in love.

Do I know what I want? I know now.

This chapter allowed me to see that I'm running after someone, something, "trying" to belong. Making, fixing, chasing something that feels right. I don't want you to "fix me" and I don't want to "fix you". Heck, you're perfect the way you are and the way you're not.

Settling for "Miss Right," last name Now, "Miss Right Now", when "Miss Right," last name For me, "Miss Right For Me" can appear any moment.

I longed for a Mermaid who would walk with me, converse with me, be happy with me, create with me; and so, these questions I pose for myself.

How do I look at a MERMAID?

Am I curiously interested in who she is?

Am I to be with this mermaid to love and to hold and to empower each other, or to use and utilize her for my needs, to be used for her needs?

I am missing the important part of having a mermaid. Which is?

To be with.

Being with someone is the most vulnerable thing that two partners unite for. Moment by moment. Just being here, now.

But the question is, do I know what I want? The answer is yes.

I've spent my life chasing after the one, hoping that I'll find someone to fix me. But not anymore. I don't need to be fixed. I don't want someone to try to "fix me." Nobody needs fixing.

I'm not the only person trying to find the one. We are all searching. We are all determined to find this perfect person. Little do we know, the one we are searching for is also searching for us.

And the one is you. It is me. It is all of us. I am the one for me, and you are the one for you. I'm talking about self-love. Self-actualization. Self-affirmation.

I don't believe we need any one person to complete us. We don't need a second half. We are whole beings, capable of doing and accomplishing anything we want. We are capable of loving ourselves.

In my search for a mythical creature, my mermaid, a legend was born. A legend named Ulrich. My LEGEND. My MYTH.

WE are our OWN Legends.

Chapter 22

MERMEN: The Word Of A Gentlemen

Growing up in a private school for boys run by monks shaped my thinking. My youth, molded by the Benedictine monks who stand by the principle, and the Latin Phrase saying, "Ora Et Labora" (Pray and Work). Standing on the three pillars of the College; Fides Scientia Virtus (Faith, Wisdom, Virtue).

My father had his own three pillars when I reached my teenage years: no drinking, no gambling, no women. "In order for you to be a great doctor," he told me, "you must refrain from drinking, gambling, and having women."
I am not a drunkard, nor a gambler, but I broke one promise out of those three agreements. I had my first "girlfriend" when I was fifteen.

My father, as you might have guessed, was a stern man. He had his own way of showing his love for my brother and I. It was tough love, but tough love is still love.

He was my first Triton, Pontus, Oceanus, and Poseidon. He didn't have a trident; he had a three-inch leather belt. I'm grateful for my father and ways, as harsh as they were. They made me who I am today. My father was the first merman I knew, but there were many others I met along my journey.

Through a mutual friend, I met a friend a playful and outgoing man, Carrot-Top Keith, as I call him. Side-by-side in our beach cleanup events, his Play Imagination team creates a strong atmosphere of fun for everyone involved.

I met another friend, Peter, who also currently works with Zero Debris. Brendan is also a leader in the organization, as well as a professional architect. Brian Patrick is a giant in the air waves. He made and gave Zero Debris fifteen minutes of fame in the airwaves, "I BE A GIANT in The Game of Snacks."

The world is full of great men and women, extraordinary human beings. Call them with a shell horn and look them in the eyes. Share what you are out to cause. They will contribute to the well-being of society. We bring "UNITY" to the word Humanity.

Chapter 21

LIVING: Rather than Surviving

*"H*ow's life?" you might ask.

I used to say, "I'm surviving." But today, I'm not surviving. I'm not just getting by.

I am living. I am grateful. I am ALIVE. I am embracing every moment.

I am present. I'm not playing on my phone all the time. I am not sustaining relationships via text message. I'm present with myself, and I'm present with all the people in my life.

I don't want to have a relationship with your texts. I'll call you, just to hear you laugh, to hear your excitement, to listen to your voice.

When someone says "I want..." all that person is doing is surviving. I don't just want. I do. I act. I create. That is how I live and enjoy life.

The marine life is surviving, as best as it can, but as you know, whales and other marine life are killed from debris, plastics, and poisoned by the man-made pollutants found inside their bellies. They are not living the way they should be.

If the world's oceans had zero debris, it would be healthy. Mother Nature takes care of her own, but right now, Mother Nature is old, tired, and she needs us to take care of her.

We've been called to act. What am I going to do about that?

To create leaders, to continue what has been started. What are you going to do about it?

To write this book and keep the awareness present. What are you going to do about that?

What are any of us going to do about the mess we've created?

I don't know about you, but I'm going to stand by what I said I'd do: to live, be alive powerfully, and to be a contribution.

I am going to clear myself of my own debris.

Chapter 20

EMERGING: One Foot Before the Other

"A journey of a thousand miles begins with a single step." (Chinese Proverb)

We often hear the term "baby steps." imagine a baby trying to walk: they stumble, they fall, they stand up again on their wobbly legs, and they try to walk again. They don't quit. They just keep getting up and trying.

What stops us from pulling ourselves up and trying again? Fear. That's all. We are afraid of greatness. The fact that I am even writing this book means I have conquered both my fear of failure and my bad habit of procrastinating.

I met an inspiring man named Bill in one of my personal development courses. This human being moved me. Bill has an amputated left leg. He was battling cancer, then he injured his leg. It became infected, and his only chance of survival was to have the infected leg amputated.

He had the surgery, his leg was amputated, and he survived. After he recovered, he started a project called Best Foot Forward, which awards scholarships to children who have lost their limbs.

It's empowering to see him eradicate the debris in his own life, to see him recover, to hear him laugh in the face of fear, and to watch him dedicate himself to the service of others. He faced down his own fear and won. I believe we can all learn from Bill's example. Lead our Best Foot Forward.

Chapter 19

The CHASE: Running Around

"*I*'m sorry, I don't have time for you, I am busy chasing something."

If we're honest, that's our usual excuse for why we can't give some of our time to others. Who knows what we're chasing? Even we don't know.

Time will never wait for us. Opportunities will be missed just because we are busy chasing. I've been chasing things ever since I was a child.

I chased the school bus, I chased my classmates on the playground, I chased the honor roll scores. I chased because I was trying to find a sense of belonging. Maybe if I get to high school, that will be it, I thought. Maybe when I get to be a dentist, that will be it. Maybe when I have a million dollars, that will be it. Maybe all those things will make me feel like I belong somewhere.

Well, I'm tired of running. I'm sweaty, weary, and exhausted.

To have zero debris in my life means I must stop the chase. I will stand on this space and create. I will create with others by sharing my life.

Never chase, for the great poet Rumi once said, "What you are seeking is seeking you."

So yes, I am tired of chasing. Tired of running. However, I never get tired of living life to the fullest. I don't chase the things I want anymore; I make them happen.

I am the possibility of being fully engaged and curiously interested in a fun loving relationship. The outcome: I have powerful relations, elated excitement, generous contribution to life.

Chapter 18

PLEASING: Do You Love Me?

I was a people-pleaser. Plain and simple. I WAS.

I've spent so many years bending over backwards to try to please partners, family members, friends, acquaintances, etc. And I've definitely been using my Zero Debris events to clean up the beaches and please Mother Earth.

I've spent too much time trying to do what other people think is right for me. It took me several years before I finally asked myself what I wanted for myself, instead of what everybody else wanted for me.

Several months ago, during one of the beach cleanups, a mermaid said to me, "Ulrich, do you know how much you are loved by these people that surround you?"

"Loved" was the word she used. Not just liked. Loved.

I smiled. "I'm glad I've made these people happy," I said, "but I no longer do things to please other people. I only do things because I want to. My CHOICE."

If I dedicated my life pleasing other people, I would lose my sense of self. I would lose my compassion for myself, I would lose my value, and I would lose my joy. Life would be a chore, an endless quest to try to live up to impossible standards.

From now on, I am only trying to please one person: Me.

Chapter 17

TOMORROW SOMEDAY: Another Day

*T*here are only seven days in the week, correct? Can you open a calendar and point out where Someday is? How about Tomorrow? Or better yet, Another Day?

Those days are fictional.

We only have this moment.

"Today was yesterday's tomorrow."

In September 2016, my 76-year-old mother fell down a small flight of stairs and broke her hip. She lives in the Philippines, and at the time, I couldn't exactly hop on a plane and fly out. No worries. all my siblings are Medical Doctors.

She received a hip replacement, and while she was recovering, I called her.

"Hello, hi,sinu ito?" she asked. ("Who is this?")

"Mama, ang pogi mong anak si Olritz po." ("Mama, your handsome son Olritz.") She says "Olritz" because Ulrich is too difficult for her to say.

"O, nahulog ako sa hagdan, eto nagrerecover na!" ("I fell down the stairs and I am recovering now.")

"That is good mama ko. Also, I wanted to say I'm sorry I can't come home to visit you. I will send you some equipment to help you heal."

"Salamat, anak. Hindi ka kelangan umuwi, bantayan mo mga apo ko. At wag kang magpapabaya. Kung magkakarun ka ng kasama o bagong asawa..."

Translation: "Thank you, my son. You don't need to come home. Take care of my grandchildren, and do not forget about yourself, if you would have a partner or a new wife." And then she started weeping.

"Opo. Wag kang mag worry, alam ko. wag ako kukuha ng picture frame, lang."

Translation: "Yes, Mama, don't worry, I know I will not get a woman who is pretty enough just to be put in a picture frame."

"Hay, naku, ang anak kong joker."

Translation: "My son, the joker." Now she was laughing. A victory.

"Mama, I am happy I've been given the chance to talk and laugh with you. I miss your cooking. I miss the vegetables you cook that I never ate."

"Oo natatandaan ko, yung munggo at ampalaya. Hay naku, puro palo ka muna bago mo kainin."

Translation: "Yes, I remember the green beans and bitter gourd. I needed to spank you in order to make you eat those vegetables."

Now we were both laughing.

"O ayan, tumatawa ka na. good. Para, pag pumanaw ka, hindi na ako iiyak, kase wala na akong tinatago, o anu man bagay na hindi ko pa na sabi at alam ko napasaya kita ngayon. kase yan lang ang mahalaga mama."

Translation: "There. You are laughing. I won't cry anymore when you leave because I haven't hidden anything from you, and there is nothing left for me to discuss, clear up, or make amends for. I know I am able to make you happy at this moment because this is what is important."

I will not wait for my my to pass away, Yes, a funeral is the highest form of acknowledgement to how a loved one has lived. People cry, for various reasons, and the truth about that is they have some unfinished business. I share with you dear readers, while you have time. Call your loved ones. Admit to things that your trash bin is loaded up.

To be clear. Not to "dump" and vomit nor to vent out. Be moved with love and have a conversation with them. Even the most trivial that you think. It will impact them and your relationship will turn towards love and forgiveness. Best of all, it will allow you to be freed up. Freedom to another level.

Sad and true, on the death bed, people can't stop crying, can't stop saying I love you and I am sorry.
The dead can not hear that.

So, I am doing it now while my mom can hear. "I can't promise you tomorrow, Mama," I said, "but I am so happy that I am given the chance to talk with you now. I love you, mama ko."

I didn't mean to say "Do not plan for tomorrow." What I was trying to communicate to my mother was that the present moment is all that matters.

At that moment, I was with my mom. I was present with her during that conversation. Nothing else mattered. I was able to silence the chatter in my head and laugh with my mother, and it felt amazing.

That is the power of living in the present.

Look, I can say "I love you" to countless women, even those who do not give a rat's ass about me, or to those who said "no, Ulrich offer that love to someone else."

So, why would I not say it to my very own mom? My own mother.

My mama. My mermaid.

So, call your mom.

You are given the chance to speak with her. How about those whose mother has passed away, six feet below the earth, or in a marble urn?

I didn't not say, "Do not plan for tomorrow." All I am saying is, this moment is what matters.

Another day perhaps?

I will throw out the garbage tomorrow. I will stop using plastic straws tomorrow. I will go to the gym tomorrow. I will start my diet tomorrow.

No, not tomorrow. Make it now.

Today, this moment is all we have.

Chapter 16

NERVOUS SMILE: The SMIRK

"Good morning."

"Hi, Good morning. How are you?" Daily pleasantries.

"What could I get for you?" asks the barista.

"I would like to have a grande in a venti cup of pike, please," is the usual answer I give.

"And your name?" she asks again.

"Ulrich."

"What?"

"UL-rich," I enunciate.

"Fulrich. Thanks." She nods.

I shake my head and give her a nervous smile.

What is a nervous smile, you ask? It's a smile that is half-hearted. I call it half-hearted because I want you to see through the bullshit, and there are indeed some people who can see through it.

My son Ethan is one of those people, and a few years ago when he was only sixteen, he gave me some advice that dramatically changed how I communicate.

I had come home from a long day of running errands, and I was stressed. Mostly due to financial concerns. Ethan noticed I was acting more preoccupied than normal.

"Dad, are you okay?" Ethan asked. "You seem stressed."

"Yeah, I'm okay, son. I just paid the rent. Also did grocery shopping," I replied.

"But are you okay?"

I gave him my typical nervous (half-hearted) smile and mustered the courage to speak the truth. "Thanks for asking, son. No, I am not okay. Thank you for your love and concern."

"You want to talk about it?"

This time, I gave him a real smile. "I am grateful that I have you as a son. Unfortunately, I cannot live up to my promise of you, me, and your brother going to the movies this weekend."

"Is that the truth?"

"Yes, it is. We only have $134.00 left in the bank until payday," I replied.

"Dad," Ethan said, "we have been through a lot, but we always manage. It is just a scratch; a flesh wound. It is not fatal. You've always told us that, no matter what, we just keep on going."

At sixteen, he was quite mature for his age.

It changed how I communicate with people, especially with my children. I want an extraordinary relationship with my kids, and I cannot have an extraordinary relationship by being inauthentic with them.

Nervous smile. No matter how the day went. This time, it is authentic, as the sparkle of the eyes, before a tear.

Chapter 15

ROUTINE: Automaticity - Default

*B*LAH BLAH BLAH.
"Hey, how are you?"
"I'm okay, I'm fine. How are you?"
"I'm doing alright."
"Good, good."
"I was meaning to ask you…."
"Alright, catch you later!"
"Bye!"

Was that a conversation?

That was a robotic conversation.

I pick up my boys from school at around 5:30-6pm DAILY, and this is how the conversation usually goes:

"Sons, did you do your homework?"

"Yes, Dad, it is already done," both Ethan and Dylan reply.

"So, where are we having dinner, guys? It's Taco Tuesday. Or we could try Pho."

"Pho, Dad," Dylan answers. (He's the one who decides where the three of us will eat because he's the pickiest eater. Ethan and I will eat just about anything.)

But what do you think? Did I just converse with my sons?

No, I didn't, that conversation was robotic BLAH BLAH BLAH.

The next day, after I pick the boys up from school, I try to engage in a more involved conversation.

"Ethan, did you participate in school today?"

"I'm part of the Junior Representatives, dad. We are kind of like legislators," he replies, and I can hear the excitement in his voice.

"Wow, really? I thought you wanted to be a forensic doctor."

"I do. This is just an extracurricular activity, dad."

"Hey, how about you, Dylan? What happened in school today? Did you recite in class?"

"Yeah, no." he replied.

"Huh?" I frowned.

He continued. "I mean, I raised my hand and..." he mumbled.

"What? I can't understand you."

"Dad, I said I raised my hand, and..." and then he trailed off again. But I didn't lose my cool, I just looked him straight in the eye and waited for him to respond.

"Dad," he repeated. "I raised my hand, and she didn't call me. She doesn't like me."

I asked him if he wanted to do a weekend seminar for youngsters. He agreed and did the seminar.

All my kids did the Transformational Learning seminar. That was my contribution to each of them, that I would introduce them to the seminars that have helped me improve myself.

None of that would have happened if I would have just carried on my typical robotic conversations. I engaged with them in that moment.

We try to spark a conversation with people, and its not with the usual pleasantries. Or else we miss the objective.

"The essence of communication is intention." (Werner Erhard)

That's the power of communication.

Chapter 14

SKEPTIC: CYNICism

*W*hen someone smiles at us, we tend to feel defensive. Once, while standing in line at my favorite coffee place, I smiled at the customer in line behind me. He just looked at me and said, "What are you smiling about?"

"Good morning," I told him.

Then he turned away.

When someone does something good for you, you become skeptical. Even cynical. They must be up to something. They must have some kind of ulterior motive, right? No one would act kindly for no reason, would they?
Yet when you give a kid something, when you do something nice for them, happiness is written all over their faces. They're not skeptical.

My father trained me. I was around thirteen or fourteen years old.

One day we went to meet some of his clients in a fancy Chinese restaurant. As soon as we entered, he told me, "Keep your eyes open and observe." So, I glanced around and scanned the entire restaurant.

Papa started with a simple question. "Do you know where the restrooms are?"

"Yes," I said.

He continued. "Do you see the woman with a blue necklace?"

"Huh?"

My eyes keenly observed, but they did not judge.

Most people would be cynical about the beach cleanup, about the Zero Debris project. Is that my problem? Is that something I am concerned about? Yes, at first. But after a while, it didn't bother me anymore. I did not concern myself with other peoples' perceptions of my passion.

One acquaintance sent me a text asking, "Bro, if I go to your beach cleanup, do I get paid?"

Fair question. I replied, "No, it's volunteer work, man."

"So, you don't get paid? How can you sustain and keep going?"

I laughed. "Bro, just come and participate. You will see."

I don't have an agenda. Like I've said, Zero Debris is more than a beach cleanup; it is a way of life.

You can be both a skeptic and a cynic and question things. You can assume the worst, if you want. But that choice is always yours.

Chapter 13

PERFECTiOn: OCD-ism

*D*ental appointment, anyone? It's time for your six-month checkup. At least, it was for my mom.

"Open wide," I told her. "A little more...the tooth is almost totally extracted."

I was extracting her upper right molar. She was smiling, numb, after being injected with Lidocaine.

"Tapos na ba?" she asked. "Na injection mo na ba ko?" Translated: "Is it done? Have you anesthetized me?"

"Yeah ma opo. I already injected you with anesthetic. Now just sit down and relax."

"Wow, wala akong naramdaman." Translated: "Wow, I didn't feel the injection."

At the time of this particular surgery, I was twenty-six years old, and my mom was my first patient.

"Syempre, naman, anesthesia nga, so wala ka talagang mararamdaman," I joked. Translation: "But of course! It's anesthesia. You wouldn't feel anything."

In the Philippines, we didn't take x-rays of the teeth. We utilized "tactile sense." Yeah, maybe it might be old school and very risky, but that was how I learned to do it.

And I wanted to do it perfectly.

The tooth was badly worn out, and I knew only a root canal could save it.

The tooth fractured. One of the roots was stuck inside the socket. The tooth extraction was not going to be as easy as I had hoped.

I made a face. I stopped singing. I was not in a fun mood anymore.

"Anak." My mom held my hand. Translated: "Son."

"Mom?"

"Kaya mo yan," she replied. Translated: "You can do it."

PerfecTioNism.

Yeah the capitalization isn't perfect. But it doesn't upset me. Not one bit. The world (and this book) is perfect as it is.

When I'm in my dental office with a patient, the first thing I check is the instrument tray. I'm checking to see if I have all my equipment in its proper place. Then I make sure the patient is properly draped, the room is well-lit, and that I have an assistant standing by.

No matter how perfect my preparation might be, there is always a small margin of error. There is always the risk of imperfection, because nothing is perfect.

Did you know dimples in a person's cheeks are an imperfection? Same as a cleft chin. A person's imperfection is what makes him or her perfect.

So be gentle with yourself. I am perfect the way I am, and the way I am not; and you are perfect the way you are and the way you are not.

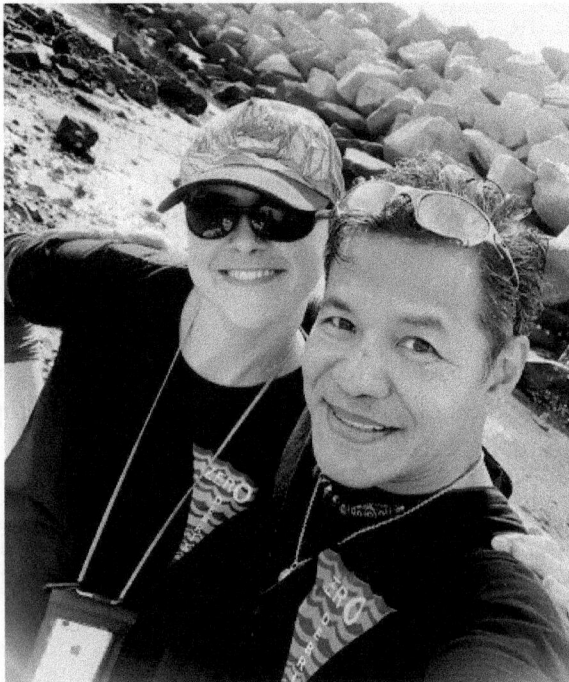

Chapter 12

THE FRIDGE: A Storage For Debris

Nowadays, most social media posts and discussions are centered around being healthy: how to eat right, counting calories, carbohydrates, protein, vitamins enriched food, fruits, what not to eat, etc.

I took a good look at what I put in my own fridge: beer, soda, eggs, celery, carrots, cakes, ketchup, dressing, comfort food (chocolate), a half-empty bottle of red wine, and cheese to go with it.

What a mess. I shook my head and started to toss things out. I then bought some cleaning supplies, filled a bucket with soap and water, and wiped down the inside.

I looked at the bottles of beer. At that point, I hadn't had a drink in over two months. Why did I still have it? I was not a drinker anymore.
Anyway, I don't need beer to have fun. So I tossed it out with the rest of my debris. And before I knew it, my fridge was cleared!

Then I moved on to the freezer. This was a bigger challenge. I found meat on top of meat - almost eight packs of stew cut, BBQ cut, etc. I found an old bag of chicken tenders and some spicy wings. I also saw a bag of ice, some ice cream, and a couple boxes of popsicles.

So I defrosted the freezer and started cleaning that out, too.

Once the freezer was cleared of all debris, I went to the grocery store and bought colorful, shapely, and sweet-smelling foods.

Now, I open my fridge, look inside, and I'm proud. I've cleaned out all the clutter. I've cleared out all the unhealthy foods that do nothing but cause more debris.

Zero Debris starts with who I am and what I eat.

Chapter 11

MIND-BODY: Trash Bin

*T*he human brain is like a new computer. Information in, information out. Garbage in, garbage out.

The body works the same way. What goes in must come out.

I went to the gym and hired a personal trainer. I started a twenty-day program and watched my muscles tone before my eyes. I did fifty situps and fifty push-ups. I lifted weights from thirty pounds up to a hundred and twenty pounds. I have a small frame. I am lightweight. But after that program, I became one hundred and thirty-seven pounds of pure muscle.

Honestly, I went to the gym for the wrong reasons. I was lifting weights and toning my muscles because I wanted to impress a woman. I was trying to impress someone else, and I didn't really care about improving my health.

Wrong reasons. What made it wrong for me is this: my body will be with me until the day I die.

If I truly wanted to improve my health, I would have quit smoking. It's a nasty habit.

I have cut down on smoking significantly, thanks to the love and support I received from my friend Jennifer D.

She reminded me that I needed to live a healthy life, so I could grow old and spend more time with my children and grandchildren.

This woman, standing for my health transformation, is a powerful woman, the voice of Asian women, actresses, and dancers in the entertainment world. Her words resounded like a gong to awaken that sixteen year old Ulrich who started smoking.

The body is a temple. My body is my own sacred sanctuary. It's the only body I have, the only body I will ever have, and I must respect it.

Chapter 10

CANCER: Cell Debris

On Superbowl Sunday 2016, I received a phone call from my ex-wife. She was very upset, almost to the point of tears. She asked me to come over to her new place, where she lived with her new husband.

Right then, her husband picked up the phone and said, "I want you to head over here. We have something to talk about." My gut feeling told me he was drunk, and that this talk would not go well.

I drove over to their place. It was a six-hour drive from my home, and I spent all six of those hours yelling, cussing, and hitting the dashboard.
When I arrived at my ex-wife's home, I saw the boys and some torn pieces of paper. The front room was silent. There was a gloomy mood.

"Good that you're here," my ex's new husband said.

"Thank you, Joe," I said, taking a seat on their couch. I was trying to follow the training I received in my personal development programs, which taught me to never bring any preconceived emotions into a conversation.

My two sons sat on my right. On my left sat my ex-wife, and directly in front of me stood Joe.

Joe spoke up. "So, your son Dylan did three things that have totally made me angry. First, he hid my under the mattress. For a week, I couldn't find them. Then he hid my phone under the CPU tower of my computer. For a week, I didn't have a phone. Lastly, he broke a bottle of very expensive cologne."

Smiling faintly, I looked at Dylan. "May I talk with my son?" Joe nodded.

"Son," I said, "are you doing these things because you want your mom and I to get back together? I'm sorry, but that won't happen."

Dylan started sniffling. So did my ex.

"Did you know," I continued, "that at this moment, there are three people who love you? Your stepdad, your mom, and me."

Now both Dylan and my ex-wife were bawling.

In that moment, I forgot Joe's anger, his heated tone, and the reason for this meeting. I was there, present in that moment, and all I felt was love for my son.

I stood up and looked Joe in the eye. I shook his hand.

"Thank you," I said, "for loving your wife the way I could not love her. Thank you for being a good father to my sons when I am not around."
Joe choked up when he said, "Let's go outside and have a cigarette."

And we did.

It could have been messy. I could have gotten angry at Joe. I could have let my own guilt and resentment consume me. But I didn't.

Resentment is a cancer. Anger, jealousy, insecurity, hate - these are cancerous emotions, and they can destroy us just as quickly as cancer destroys the cells in our bodies.

That day, my boys had the opportunity to see a different father. They saw a Papa who was not as angry as he once was.

On Superbowl Sunday 2016, I took my first step to clearing the debris of resentment from my heart. Shift the act of listening with freedom to express one's love. Happiness and Peace.

The Zero Debris team invited Judy Lee to be the guest speaker for the event.

I honor this woman and I always have high regards to her. She was my leader coach on projects. You know how this powerful loving woman got me started on my self-expression of what contribution I can share? Judy Lee asked me one question. "What lights you up?, young man?"

What lights you up?

That is a profound question.

What gives you joy? the spark, the juice, the smile the laughter the blissfulness.

What gives you light? What are you passionate about?

"What lights me up, coach? It lights me up when I sing. Yes, I love karaoke." I smiling replied

"There, start there, Look and see what project can come out from that. Apply and use the distinctions of the program." my loving coach said.

So a new cell is formed. If cancer is a dreadful disease, there are powerful men and women who battle this disease amidst pain, discomfort, and against financial obligation, against resignation.

They even have a smile, a pure one if I may add.

The ocean water is sick, let us not wait for it to be like a 4th stage of cancer before we start cleaning it.

Chapter 9

DOCTORS / PATIENTS: Vice Versa

As a child, when I caught a cold or a flu, my Papa would come up to my bed, wake me up and say, "Bangon na, huwag mong bebaby ang sakit mo." Translated: "Rise up, and don't treat your sickness like a baby."

He was a doctor who practiced tough love.

Even now, I seldom take a leave of absence from work. Except when I suffer from gout, which comes from too much beer, red meat, or whatever it is that triggers uric acid to accumulate in my system.

When I am sick, I am a patient. Yes, doctors also get sick.

That doctor-patient relationship demonstrates that, as humans, we need each other. Not all patients need medication in the form of a pill. Some patients just need someone to talk to, someone to hold their hand, someone to joke with, etc.

A person who is kind, loving, and generous is also a doctor. We are all doctors and patients to someone. Our first doctors are our Father and Mother. Our first patients are our siblings, grand parents.

Imagine: let's say the beach is the hospital and you came to meditate and heal. Can you heal and meditate with all that trash around you? Would you like to sit down and get poked by a broken bottle?

Would you go back to a hospital that is septic? Would you go back to a hospital where the doctors, nurses, and assistants were unprofessional?

Would you go back to a beach that is littered?

Let us be doctors of the beach.

Not for our sake, but for the marine life living in the ocean.

We, the Zero Debris team, are doctors, nursing the beach, the harbor, the marina, and the sea creatures back to health by cleaning their habitat. We are also patients who need to feel the ocean breeze. We need to listen to the soothing waves.

That is what heals us.

Chapter 8

PROGNOSIS: Worse, Fair, Good

A good friend of mine once told me, "Bro, this Zero Debris thing you started is like a band-aid being placed on the world."

"Thank you," I told him, "but the Zero Debris team is not placing a band-aid over Mother Earth's wounds. The Zero Debris team is actually exposing the wound."

That's the truth. We are exposing the wound so people will know the extent of how we have damaged the planet. Zero Debris is not a band-aid; it is a call to action.

Mother Earth is sick, and her prognosis is will continue to get worse, unless we all join together and create a massive change.

I've always been adamant about doing this. I live for my word. I believe, without a doubt, that my team will make an impact on the world. I believe we can change it for the better.

Recently, I had a short heart-to-heart conversation with Pattie, my publisher.

"I'm not sure what you've started, Ulrich," she said, "I admire your passion, I admire your heart and this will be your legacy."

"Thank you, I appreciate your acknowledgement" my heartfelt reply.

This book will keep me present. It will keep me in check and hold me to my word. It will inspire me, and hopefully you, to go out and make a change in our world.

Chapter 7

SURRENDER

*W*hen I say "surrender," I am not talking about giving up. Well, at least not in a bad way, because I am talking about relinquishing bad habits.

This movement started without a structure. That is what I thought.

We do have a structure. We invite, we gather, we pick up trash, we weigh the debris collected, and we generate the purpose of what Zero Debris is all about.

I'm talking about giving up my habit of being judgemental. I'm giving up my obsession with always being correct. I am giving up lying, making excuses, sabotaging myself, whining, bickering, and so much more.

I am surrendering myself to the powers of love, generosity, freedom, and service to mankind.

People get drawn to my Zero Debris team by my energy and compassion. Our beach cleanup events allow friends and teammates to demonstrate their passion for our environment.

My friend Laura started her own nonprofit called The Leroy Project. It's named after her rescue dog, Leroy. The Leroy Project is building a no-kill shelter for animals. I volunteer my time any time I can.

"Are we still talking about Zero Debris?" you ask.

Yes, we are. Animals need to be treated with love and care, too. We need to clean up our own emotional debris, and so do animals.

Zero Debris is more than just a beach cleanup. It is you. It is an effort to help you see your own debris.

I see mine, and I embrace it fully.

I surrender it. I renounce it.

Chapter 6

FAILURES / SUCCESSES

*W*hen I was eight years old, I owned a child-sized BMX bike. I was starting to learn how to ride a bike. As I rode, I looked down at my feet in order to balance myself.

No one finds balance by looking at their feet while pedaling, and sure enough, I crashed. Again and again. Time after time. I wasn't paying attention to the road, I was too busy staring down at my feet. I couldn't move past my fear of falling.

I got a lot of bruises, scrapes, and stitches from crashing on my BMX. But it was all part of the process of learning to ride a bike. Would you say I failed by crashing? Or would you say I succeeded?

It is just what you make of it.

The same rule applies to the Zero Debris movement. So far, the largest number of volunteers we've had for one event was twenty-eight. We've had a grand total of 28 people cleaning up the shoreline at once.

Have we failed? Or have we succeeded?

Well, we kept our word. We promised to:

1. Be at the Santa Monica Pier Lifeguard Tower 20 once a month. We have kept that promise.

2. To pick up debris along the shoreline. We have kept that promise, too.

3. To weigh the debris collected and tally it. The objective last year (2018) was a total of 1 tonnage of debris, 2018. We kept that promise, too.

4. To have fun while being a contribution, spreading awareness, and growing the network of participants and volunteers. (This promise is currently a work in progress, but it's happening)

Zero Debris began as two friends taking an action. We are now 136 friends and volunteers strong. According to Facebook, 278 virtual friends have liked the page.

Oh, and we made one more promise:

5. To continue this action no matter what, come rain or shine, hell or high water.

We have done this. We've never missed an event. We've never moved the date of the event. No excuses. No matter what the temperature or weather may be, we have kept our word.

Zero Debris has not failed. It is a success.

Failure is what happens if we do not keep the promises we made when we started this organization.

I will keep on playing. I will continue inviting people to attend. I will keep the sand clean and free of debris the way only us Zeroes can.

Chapter 5

ACCOMPLISHMENTS:

*H*ere lies the remains of a man who is a son, a brother, a father, a friend, a teammate, an amazing leader, a man who is pure fun, excitement, and generosity. Make the angels wear gloves while, hand in hand, you create a heaven with zero debris.

That my dear readers, would be a great epitaph. I have accomplished many things in my life.

I have created an environmental movement that has spanned the globe. I quit smoking. I put my kids through college, actually two more kiddos to go.. I wrote this book, and the most important accomplishment of all, I have created a life I love.

I won three gold medals for winning first place in three declamation contests. I won two silver medals for extemporaneous speaking over the course of three separate years.

Recently, a Zero Debris teammate, Mo, she said, "Ulrich, do you know that I thought about Zero Debris this morning? I was discarding a plastic soap dispenser that didn't have a working pump. Then I saw another plastic dispenser that had a pump. I was about to discard both of them, but I thought about you, and guess what?"

"What?" I asked.

"I ended up discarding only one. I took the pump of the other dispenser. So, instead of two plastic containers, I was able to utilize the other."

What can I say? My philosophy is really rubbing off on people. Now that is another accomplishment.

Chapter 4

TEAM and TEAM MATES

On February 10, 2019, I was supervising another Zero Debris cleanup. I stood on the sand, smiling to myself while I watched my teammates pick up rubble. About fifty paces from the canopy area, another handful of team members were taking pictures and recording videos of the event.

The team assigned to take photos and videos is headed by Tristan from Pentalated Media team.

We had set up three tents along the shore. These tents played loud, energetic music, to keep the team's morale up, and to catch the attention of any curious spectators passing through.

Some local residents stopped and read the banner. Others were daring enough to strike up a conversation with whoever was at the tent, which is usually, me, Mikel, Darren, Hamid, or Jessica.

Zero Debris is not me. It is a team; a team of generous, fun loving, humans that have a big space in their hearts to contribute their time, resources, and happy energy.

All for one mission: to clear any body of water of debris and pollutants are harmful to both humans and marine life. The Admin team, as well as loyal supporters, come to have a monthly get together.

Zero Debris has became popular with the local community. At our events, we've met so many amazing people including a photographer who takes still shots for surfers. Her name is Martha, but would like to be called "Mermaid." She has photographed several of our events.

We've met a teacher from Santa Monica High School. Professor Ben, who is also a marine biologist. He enlisted a team of high school students to help clean the beach.

So, I ask you: What is a team? What are teammates?

No peeking. Don't ask your phone.

My definition of a team is a diverse group of individuals acting as one.

I am grateful to all the men and women who have been actively present in the cause, in the movement. This book from the start talks about teammates joining together causing each other to fulfill what matters to them.

I stand by my claim that Zero Debris is not just an organization. It is a way of life.

Chapter 3

CURIOSITY: An Inquiry

I'm a curious person. And even though I have cleaned out a lot of my own personal debris, lately I've been wondering what else is in there. What other mental or emotional debris is still inside? Is there anything else still holding me back and preventing me from reaching my full potential?

It was the eve of 4th of July. As the day unfolded, it was mid-morning, when I read the email from a co-team mate of mine, scheduled for a conference call via a meeting room at noon.

I dialed in and there she was. "Hey, Joey," I said. "Hi Ulrich. You're driving. Are you going to the beach?" She smiled.

"No, I am heading to a meeting," I replied. "Great, it is because I always associate you with the beach," she joked.

We both chuckled.

"Joey, as you can see, I have my hands on the wheel," I said, while raising my hands to show her. We both were belly aching with laughter.

"So, is it just me and you on this con-call?" I asked.

"Looks like it," was her reply.

Out of curiosity, I asked, "What are you up to in this game of life?"

"I am in search of complete health and wellness. I took time off to re-evaluate, relearn, and restructure my being, to be in the healthy state of my life. So, now it is time for me to be out and discover, inquire, and be curious." Her eyes lit up and she had a big smile fixed upon her lovely face.

"The curious feline," I remarked.

As she was putting her hair in a ponytail, I wondered about what she was sharing and what she wanted in her life, and it led me to share.

I told her that Zero Debris was more than a beach clean up. It was about me removing all of my own debris so I can be a contribution to the world. She was awed by that. "You're right," she agreed.

She has attended a lot of spiritual retreats and meditations because she is very curious what her life is all about. Her health and wellness a year and a half ago was in question.

Her sharing shifted my thinking. I was curious what else was under the rug that I hadn't cleared out?

Curious as I continue searching for my own debris.

Curious as to what I missed out on, to look at. Is there anything in my being that is holding me back in being totally zilch with trash?

I asked if she would want to read chapters of my book during the book signing. "Yes," she said, "I would love to."

Then I noticed, because of this topic, I myself became curious. "Why Joey? I mean, what's in your name?"

She's named after a great ballet dancer, Joey Heatherton.

There is a story behind our names. Each and every human we've met has a reason for their name.

Because of this conversation with Joey; I was curious about my own name, and I recently spoke on the phone with my father. I had a question for him.

"Papa, out of curiosity, why did you name me Ulrich?"

"Because," he replied, "in the book of baby boy names, Ulrich is a norse name meaning noble ruler."

"I am glad to know that, Papa," I smiled.

Instead of living my life frantically; instead of feeling rushed, distracted, and disconnected all the time, I've chosen to change. I've learned to shift my mindset. I've learned to calm myself, to make myself available, interested, and curious.

When we are curious and inquire about things, it usually comes from a place of concern. It comes from a place of trying to receive an answer, from a desire to learn new information. My story about asking my father the reason for my name might sound trivial, but it is not. Curiosity comes in all shapes and sizes.

I have big curiosity in my vision for Zero Debris. I envision being curiously interested, engaged, and living in a fun-loving, free and clean environment. I envision a powerful circle of generous kind-hearted, and service-based leaders.

This vision, and my curiosity gives me a sweet smile on my face as I type and continue to finish this book. A life with zero debris is a utopia. It may or may not happen; however, I am happy to know that at least I will live my life free of much of the debris from within and around me.

Can I give you some advice? Don't listen to that old expression, "Curiosity killed the cat."

It might not be true. Curiosity doesn't always kill. Sometimes it can make you laugh, sometimes it teaches you things and introduces you to different points of view.

Chapter 2

PUZZLE: A Piece I Hold

*W*e are all connected as part of the human race. Regardless of age, gender, religion, political affiliation, or any other superficial label, we are deeply connected to each other.

At the end of one's life, we are DEBRIS as well. We are made from debris, don't forget that. A heap of debris, dust, a speck in a vast universe.

Every person is one piece of a larger puzzle. We are designed to connect with other pieces. A child's puzzle does not have only one large piece. Neither does the puzzle of humanity. We are meant to connect.

I have connected with hundreds of people since Zero Debris began.

The Zero Debris team consists of people who might not fit together outside of this movement, but we all share the same goal of improving the environment. Listen your world, as KellyAnn would say. A Giant with a big piece of the puzzle, asking you and me, to listen, the world is saying something.

Some people join Zero Debris for a little while and then leave. Some have stayed on as permanent members of the team. No matter who we are as individuals, no matter which country we live in, the Zero Debris team is united as one.

We are all part of a larger puzzle: the puzzle called Life.

Chapter 1

One Plus Zero Is A HERO

*T*he number zero means nothing, right? By itself, it has no value. Zero only has power when another number is added to it.

Put the number one in front of zero, and it becomes ten. Put another zero at the end of that number, and ten becomes one hundred. Put another zero after that, and one hundred becomes one thousand. You get the idea.

One is a prime number. Being number one is a good thing. Yet, being number one is also a lonely thing.

Imagine if I was the only one cleaning up the beaches. I would have given up by now. It would have been a fad.

Thankfully, that is not the case. I am not the only one cleaning the beaches. I have the support and companionship of an entire team.

We, the Zero Debris team, affectionately call ourselves Zeroes. And we all have incredible power. We are curious and passionate individuals who are making a difference in this world, one plastic bottle at a time.

A zero is a circular shape. It has no beginning and no end. No limitations. Its value is limitless. Just like my value is limitless. And so is yours.

Now, what are you going to do about that?

Chapter 0

Zero Debris Is More Than A Beach Cleanup

This is not an ending.

This is a beginning.

This is the start of a new chapter in my life. I'm looking back at the debris that is still inside me, and I am giving myself a choice. I only have one life, and I am choosing to pursue the life that I want for myself.

I encourage you to do the same.

Give yourself a fresh start, a choice. Admit that you have debris. Rid yourself of your debris. You will notice the change.

Commence. To value the planet we live in. To value each and every living human being as well as the natural resources we have. This book has lit me up, brought me to tears, gave me compassion for what I have done and what I have yet to do. It has allowed to embrace the humanity inside of myself, as well as others.

May this book provide you a deeper insight into yourself, your family, friends, and for the rest of society.

I am Ulrich. Together with the Zero Debris team, I am signing on.

Acknowledgments:

*I*f this were a movie, you would be watching credits right now.

Please stay for those credits. Kindly read everything because there will be a post-credits scene, a preview of what the next book will be. It is also because I do not want to overlook anybody, and if I do miss anyone, I apologize for it. Let's just say, it was a glitch.

To the mandibulate arthropods, shrimps and lobsters subphylum Crustacea: for nibbling on the microplastics we irresponsibly dispose.

To the whales: your species has swallowed more than enough debris than your bellies can hold.

To the sea turtles: your species has endured getting trapped within our plastics.

To the charadriiformes (sea birds): your species has been trapped in oil spills.

To the transformational coaches and leaders of Landmark Worldwide: I have taken these courses for my own personal and professional development. Specially, I'd like to thank to Judy Lee Chen Seng. This woman first proposed the idea that I should go pick up bottles on the shoreline.

To Jen Herda, the leader who is generously open and stands for every team member fully reaching a transformed life in communication.

To Jerry Burkhard Center Manager and Forum leader LA Landmark Worldwide, who inspires me to be a man of my word.

To Michelle Ratmansky, my friend, client, and amazing human being. Thank you for your love, support, and whooping my ass from time to time and calling my BS. I love you so much. Regards to your mother, the queen.

To our first ever donors and sponsors: Marisol Benavides and her son, Richie Herrera. You both have hearts filled with love. You are the ones who solidified the Zeroes by granting us our first tent and canopy. Thank you for your generosity and contribution. God bless you.

To my editor Brianna Rose Burton, for her candid, bubbly personality, and her strength in enduring my quirks. I appreciate you. I cannot thank you enough. Thanks for signing the NDA.

To my Mama Adelia and Papa Leto, whose love is unyielding. To my brother Herbert, who has always believed in me. To my sisters Clarissa, Clarabelle, and Euphemia, who showed me how powerful women are.

To my kids, Ariadne, Ethan, and Dylan: my nurse, my future doctor, and my paleontologist. From day one, you have all fully supported me in my mission. You have inspired me daily, and you continue to do so. You have touched my life with a dash of laughter, a sprinkle of love, and a scoop of honey.

To Abigail Gazda, a life coach, podcaster, leader, and the woman who inspired me to get out of my comfort zone and begin the Zero Debris project.

To Play Imagination, headed by Keith Vogel. I salute you. You are the only red-haired Filipino. Thank you for allowing me to play my childhood games with you. Awesome sauce.

To the Zero Debris team, Hamid, Jessica, Mikel and Darren: I love you guys. Thank you for your unwavering support.

To the Zero Debris Philippine team, Hector Joseph Raphael and Chit Dhan, for saying YES to a cause without even knowing how it would turn out.

To the Zero Debris Mexico team, Angeles Clemente, Israel and more amigos and amigas than I can count. Gracias. Thank you for your leadership and generosity.

To NJ Zajac, the kween of Redondo Harbor's Paddle4Plastic. You always amaze me with your love, your support, and your countless contributions to Zero Debris. We will always have fun, and you still owe me a home cooked meal of "vegan" food. I owe you one Filipino Dish. Let us paddle4plastic until there is Zero Debris!

To Team Marine, headed by Professor Benjamin Kay, and the Santa Monica High School students. Thank you for contributing to the cause. We are grateful. I am grateful. The ocean is grateful.

To The countless men, women, and children who participate in our monthly events. I am very grateful.

To New Life Clarity Publishing, Pattie Sadler, the woman who supported me, after only two minutes of speaking. I'm looking forward to working on other projects with you.

To Kelsey, for your devotion and talent. I appreciate you.

To my editor Matt: Bro, I think you are my reflection. Thanks for doing an awesome job! You guys are officially part of the Zero Debris team!

To Kindle Publishing and Amazon Publishing Company, for helping me market and spread awareness of this book. I am grateful for your assistance.

To the mermaids and mermen who created this book with me, I am grateful.

To my one and only mermaid, for giving me the light on my path to forge this mission, and for making sure I remain a man of my word.

For the love and compassion; for understanding me in moments and times I didn't understand myself; for the unwavering pillar of peace amidst the uncertainty. You have swam with me against currents, against waves. You are my strength, as I am yours. I am very grateful.

I acknowledge you for who you are, for your contribution, your generosity, for the unrelenting power of words.

I appreciate you for purchasing this book. 50% of this book's earnings will be donated to the non-profit organization, Zero Debris.

I acknowledge the One who made the seas, the land, the air and its beautiful creatures. I acknowledge the One who gave me life, the one who gave me everyone I love. To the one who believed in me first, by creating my being: thank you, my God.

Thank you. Salamat po. My grateful heart will always acknowledge your contribution.

Chapter 49

The Deep Blue Sea: The Saga Continues.

The man who married a mermaid stood alone on the beach, watching the sunrise. It had been almost three decades since he had fallen in love with his mermaid. They had married, separated, divorced, as many people do, and now he was alone on the shore.

He stood in the exact spot he had made his promise to the merman king. He had given his word to clean the beaches of all the debris humans had left.

He sat down on the sand, and noticed a piece of plastic stuck underneath. He shook his head. Digging deep, he pulled the plastic bag out of the sand, stood up, and decided to do something about it.

He was about thirty minutes into picking up trash when he looked around and saw several people doing the same. More and more people joined in.

The man began cheering for them. "Woohoo! Keep going, everyone! Let's do this until there is zero debris!"

Then, he started to chant. The chanting continued until the whole beachfront sang in unison. By now, it was almost noon. Dump trucks arrived to haul all the debris away.

He looked out towards the ocean, and there, in the distance, she emerged: his mermaid. She was still wearing her wedding dress.

Weeping, the man knelt down on the sand. His heart pounded as she approached him.

She knelt in front of him and placed her right hand on his wrinkled face. She placed her left hand against his heart.

"I'm sorry," she said. "It took me thirty years to realize that I love you. I love you even more than the sea."

After a pause, he spoke. "I have missed you so much. I have never loved anyone since you. I love you and only you."

The princess' eyes filled with tears. "I am now going to give you a choice. Come join me beneath the waves and sit by my side as my husband. But know this: after I am crowned queen, I cannot resurface and leave my domain."

He was anxious. Was he ready for this? What about the life on the surface he would be leaving behind? How could he survive underwater?

"Princess." He held her face with both hands. "May I kiss you?"

She nodded. He leaned in and kissed her on the lips. As they kissed, his feet began transforming. Webbing spread between his toes, as well as his fingers. The people on the shore started cheering.

He stopped kissing the mermaid, turned around, and addressed the crowd. "Continue what we have begun, my friends! I will come back once every month and assist you."

The mermaid and merman began walking into the water. After a few moments, they disappeared beneath the water together, while the crowd on the beach continued to cheer.

BOOK 2

Chapter 50

BLANK SLATE.

In a space of nothingness...
... Anything is possible..

About The Author

Ulrich Floresca

Ulrich Floresca is a massage therapist and former dentist who, since his 48th birthday; has been living an entirely new way of life. A life of Zero Debris. When he turned 48, Ulrich chose to improve himself and the world by taking on doing 48 Acts of Love & Kindness, which quickly turned into a monthly international beach cleanup and him becoming a published author.

Although Ulrich's love of writing started when he was a teenager, using poetry to woo the ladies; it has since become an incredibly powerful tool. He now uses his passion, writing & voice to free himself & others from the debris that holds them back, both internally and externally.

Ulrich is looking to collaborate with people around the globe to make a profound difference for Mother Earth, and to help fulfill his utopian vision. His non-profit organization currently spans 3 countries and is growing rapidly. He aims to expand Zero Debris so that each country and each world citizen can enjoy the benefits of having a clean internal and external environment.

www.zer0debris.org/

www.ingramcontent.com/pod-product-compliance
Lightning Source LLC
Chambersburg PA
CBHW060044030426
42334CB00019B/2486